GoodFood
Make-ahead meals

D0246230

10 9 8 7 6 5 4 3 2 1

Published in 2012 by BBC Books, an imprint of Ebury Publishing
A Random House Group company

Photographs © BBC Worldwide 2012
Recipes © BBC Worldwide 2012
Book design © Woodlands Books Ltd 2012
All recipes contained in this book first appeared in BBC *Good Food* magazine.

The Random House Group Limited
Reg. No. 954009

Addresses for companies within the Random House Group can be found at www.randomhouse.co.uk

A CIP catalogue record for this book is available from the British Library

The Random House Group Limited supports The Forest Stewardship Council® (FSC®), the leading international forest certification organisation. Our books carrying the FSC label are printed on FSC® certified paper. FSC is the only forest certification scheme endorsed by the leading environmental organisations, including Greenpeace. Our paper procurement policy can be found at www.randomhouse.co.uk/environment

To buy books by your favourite authors and register for offers visit www.randomhouse.co.uk

Printed and bound by Firmengruppe APPL, aprinta druck, Wemding, Germany
Colour origination by Dot Gradations Ltd, UK

Commissioning Editor: Muna Reyal
Project Editor: Joe Cottington
Designer: Kathryn Gammon
Production: Lucy Harrison
Picture Researcher: Gabby Harrington

ISBN: 9781849904698

Picture credits

BBC *Good Food* magazine and BBC Books would like to thank the following people for providing photos. While every effort has been made to trace and acknowledge all photographers, we should like to apologise should there be any errors or omissions.

Marie-Louise Avery p117; Carolyn Barber p33, p103, p127; Peter Cassidy p55, p119, p131, p161, p171, p187, p191; Jean Cazals p143, p169; Will Heap p21, p37, p65, p67, p81, p93; Sian Irvine p69; Gareth Morgans p39, p85, p111, p159; David Munns p19, p25, p31, p43, p47, p59, p75, p77, p83, p91, p95, p101, p115, p129, p135, p145, p165, p175, p189, p193, p205; Myles New p17, p23, p27, p79, p97, p105, p107, p109, p137, p139, p141, p147, p149, p179, p181, p185, p195, p197, p199, p201, p203; Stuart Ovenden p11; Lis Parsons p29, p57, p71, p73, p121, p151, p157, p167, p177; Charlie Richards p49, p51, p53, p209; Maja Smend p13, p99; Brett Stevens p125; Roger Stowell p123, p133; Yuki Sugiura p15, p41, p63, p153; Debi Treloar p113, p173; Simon Walton p35; Philip Webb p45, p61, p87, p89, p155, p163, p183, p207, p211

All the recipes in this book were created by the editorial team at *Good Food* and by regular contributors to BBC magazines.

weekend

GoodFood
Make-ahead meals

Editor **Barney Desmazery**

BOOKS

Contents

Introduction

Want to know the secret to stress-free entertaining? Want to know how you can eat home-cooked food on a weeknight when you don't have time to make it? The answer is make it ahead.

Cooking ahead, whether it's big batch or simply throwing something together for later when you won't have the time or the inclination, saves you money and is much healthier for you than a microwaved ready-meal or last-minute take-away.

Obviously making food ahead takes a degree of planning, which is why we came up with this book to help you. Packed with dishes for weeknight suppers or dinner parties, every recipe can be at the least assembled ahead of time, leaving you only a little last-minute cooking, while many can be completely made ahead, leaving you nothing but a bit of reheating to do.

Another important element to making food ahead is freezing, so we have included a whole chapter dedicated to food for the freezer, and elsewhere a freezer symbol at the top of each recipe clearly indicates if the dish can be frozen, with advice on when in the method to do this and for how long.

As ever, all our recipes are triple-tested in our test kitchen – and that includes freezing instructions as well. So make time for yourself another day and get into the kitchen and make those meals ahead!

Barney

Notes and conversion tables

NOTES ON THE RECIPES
• Eggs are large in the UK and Australia and extra large in America unless stated otherwise.
• Wash fresh produce before preparation.
• Recipes contain nutritional analyses for 'sugar', which means the total sugar content including all natural sugars in the ingredients, unless otherwise stated.

❄ SUITABLE FOR FREEZING
Some of the recipes in this book are perfect for freezing, and so we've marked them with this symbol. Unless otherwise stated, freeze for up to three months. Defrost thoroughly and heat until piping hot.

OVEN TEMPERATURES

Gas	°C	°C Fan	°F	Oven temp.
¼	110	90	225	Very cool
½	120	100	250	Very cool
1	140	120	275	Cool or slow
2	150	130	300	Cool or slow
3	160	140	325	Warm
4	180	160	350	Moderate
5	190	170	375	Moderately hot
6	200	180	400	Fairly hot
7	220	200	425	Hot
8	230	210	450	Very hot
9	240	220	475	Very hot

APPROXIMATE WEIGHT CONVERSIONS
• All the recipes in this book list both imperial and metric measurements. Conversions are approximate and have been rounded up or down. Follow one set of measurements only; do not mix the two.
• Cup measurements, which are used by cooks in Australia and America, have not been listed here as they vary from ingredient to ingredient. Kitchen scales should be used to measure dry/solid ingredients.

SPOON MEASURES

Spoon measurements are level unless otherwise specified.

- 1 teaspoon (tsp) = 5ml
- 1 tablespoon (tbsp) = 15ml
- 1 Australian tablespoon = 20ml (cooks in Australia should measure 3 teaspoons where 1 tablespoon is specified in a recipe)

APPROXIMATE LIQUID CONVERSIONS

metric	imperial	AUS	US
50ml	2fl oz	¼ cup	¼ cup
125ml	4fl oz	½ cup	½ cup
175ml	6fl oz	¾ cup	¾ cup
225ml	8fl oz	1 cup	1 cup
300ml	10fl oz/½ pint	½ pint	1¼ cups
450ml	16fl oz	2 cups	2 cups/1 pint
600ml	20fl oz/1 pint	1 pint	2½ cups
1 litre	35fl oz/1¾ pints	1¾ pints	1 quart

Good Food is concerned about sustainable sourcing and animal welfare. Where possible humanely reared meats, sustainably caught fish (see fishonline.org for further information from the Marine Conservation Society) and free-range chickens and eggs are used when recipes are originally tested.

Chunky sweetcorn, haddock & potato soup

Serve up a satisfying meal in a bowl with this sumptuous smoked-fish soup.

❄ • **TAKES 35 MINUTES** • **SERVES 4**

25g/1oz butter
1 onion, chopped
8 rashers smoked streaky bacon,
    chopped
3 medium potatoes, diced
1 litre/1¾ pints vegetable stock
2 sweetcorn cobs, kernels sliced off
500g/1lb 2oz skinless smoked haddock,
    cut into bite-size pieces
5 tbsp double cream
small bunch parsley, chopped
crusty bread, to serve

1 Melt the butter in a large pan. Fry the onion and bacon for 5 minutes until soft. Add the potatoes to the pan and cook for a further 2 minutes, then pour in the stock and simmer for 8 minutes or until the potatoes are just tender.

2 Add the corn kernels and smoked haddock. Cook for another 3 minutes then add the double cream and some black pepper. Taste before you add any salt. The soup can now be chilled for up to 2 days or frozen for a month. If freezing, defrost completely before reheating gently in a pan. When the soup is hot, stir through the chopped parsley. Ladle into bowls and serve with crusty bread, if you like.

PER SERVING 484 kcals, protein 35g, carbs 27g, fat 27g, sat fat 13g, fibre 4g, sugar 6g, salt 4.4g

Beetroot houmous

This freezable houmous is a great way of using up a glut of beetroot and makes a vibrant, healthy snack. Make a big batch and freeze half for another time.

❄ • **TAKES 1 HOUR** • **SERVES 8**

500g/1lb 2oz raw beetroot, leaves trimmed to 2.5cm/1in, but root left whole
2 × 400g cans chickpeas, drained and rinsed
juice 2 lemons
1 tbsp ground cumin
yogurt, toasted cumin seeds, mint leaves and crusty bread, to serve

1 Cook the beetroot in a large pan of boiling water with the lid on for 30–40 minutes until tender. When they're done, a skewer or knife should go all the way in easily. Drain, then set aside to cool.

2 Pop on a pair of rubber gloves. Pull off and discard the roots, leaves, stalk and skin of the cooled beetroot. Roughly chop the flesh. In a food processor, whizz the beetroot, chickpeas, lemon juice, cumin, 2 teaspoons salt and some pepper. The houmous can now be chilled and left in the fridge to dip into for up to 3 days or frozen for a month. Defrost completely if frozen and serve swirled with a little yogurt, some toasted cumin seeds, a little torn mint and some crusty bread.

PER SERVING 90 kcals, protein 6g, carbs 15g, fat 1g, sat fat none, fibre 4g, sugar 5g, salt 1.69g

Best-ever chunky guacamole

As long as you cover the surface of the guacamole with a good squeeze of lime it can be made the day before without browning.

TAKES 15 MINUTES ● SERVES 8

1 large ripe tomato
3 avocados, very ripe but not bruised
juice 2 limes
handful coriander, leaves and stalks
    chopped, plus a few leaves, roughly
    chopped, to garnish (optional)
1 small red onion, finely chopped
1 chilli, red or green, deseeded and
    finely chopped
tortilla chips, to serve

1 Use a large knife to pulverise the tomato to a pulp on a board, then tip into a bowl. Halve and stone the avocados (saving a stone) and use a spoon to scoop out the flesh into the bowl with the tomato.

2 Tip half the lime juice and all the other ingredients (except the tortilla chips) into the bowl, then season with some salt and pepper. Use a whisk to roughly mash everything together. If you are preparing ahead, flatten the surface with the back of a spoon, drizzle with the remaining lime juice and sit an avocado stone in the guacamole (this helps to stop it going brown). Cover with cling film and chill until needed – it will keep at its best until the next day.

3 When ready to serve, give the guacamole a good stir, scatter with the coriander, if using, then serve with tortilla chips.

PER SERVING 103 kcals, protein 1g, carbs 2g, fat 10g, sat fat 1g, fibre 2g, sugar 0g, salt 0.01g

Smoked salmon taramasalata

If you are being budget conscious, this delicious dip can be made with the cheaper packs of smoked salmon trimmings you find next to the slices.

TAKES 10 MINUTES ● SERVES 4

100g/4oz smoked salmon
200g/7oz low-fat cream cheese
100ml/3½fl oz crème fraîche
juice 1 lemon
cracked pepper
drizzle of olive oil
Kalamata olives and griddled pitta
  bread, to serve

1 Tip the salmon, cream cheese, crème fraiche and lemon juice into a food processor and blitz everything until smooth, then stir in the cracked pepper.
2 Spoon the mix into a large bowl, cover with cling film and chill for up to 3 days.
3 To serve, drizzle with olive oil and eat with griddled pitta bread and some kalamata olives.

PER SERVING 203 kcals, protein 14g, carbs 2g, fat 15g, sat fat 10g, fibre none, sugar 2g, salt 1.80g

10-minute couscous salad

This makes a great lunch-box filler for a day out and is equally good at home from the fridge.

TAKES 10 MINUTES • SERVES 2

100g/4oz couscous
200ml/7fl oz hot low-salt vegetable
    stock (from a cube is fine)
2 spring onions
1 red pepper, deseeded
½ cucumber
2 tbsp pesto
50g/2oz feta, cubed
2 tbsp toasted pine nuts

1 Tip the couscous into a large bowl and pour over the stock. Cover, then leave for 10 minutes, until fluffy and all the stock has been absorbed.
2 Meanwhile, slice the onions and pepper and dice the cucumber. Add these to the couscous, fork through the pesto, crumble in the feta and mix well. The salad will now keep in the fridge for up to 2 days.
3 Sprinkle over the pine nuts to serve.

PER SERVING 327 kcals, protein 13g, carbs 33g, fat 17g, sat fat 5g, fibre 2g, sugar 7g, salt 0.88g

Zingy salmon & brown rice salad

Make this superhealthy salad for a dinner for two and take the leftovers to work the next day. Your colleagues will be so jealous!

TAKES 40 MINUTES ● SERVES 3–4

200g/7oz brown basmati rice
200g/7oz frozen soya beans, defrosted
2 salmon fillets
1 cucumber, diced
small bunch spring onions, sliced
small bunch coriander, roughly
    chopped
zest and juice 1 lime
1 red chilli, diced (deseeded, if you
    prefer)
4 tsp light soy sauce

1 Cook the rice according to the pack instructions, and 3 minutes before it's done, add the soya beans. Drain and cool under cold running water.

2 Meanwhile, put the salmon on a plate, then microwave on High for 3 minutes or until cooked through. Allow to cool slightly, remove the skin with a fork, then flake.

3 Gently fold the cucumber, spring onions, coriander and salmon into the rice and beans. In a separate bowl, mix the lime zest and juice, chilli and soy, then pour over the rice before serving. The salad will keep in the fridge for up to 2 days, just give it a stir before serving.

PER SERVING (3) 497 kcals, protein 34g,
carbs 61g, fat 15g, sat fat 3g, fibre 5g, sugar 6g,
salt 1.42g

Asian chicken salad

Turn this salad into a packed lunch with a difference, or make it up the night before and dress it just before eating. It also works with cooked prawns instead of chicken.

TAKES 20 MINUTES ● SERVES 2

1 boneless skinless chicken breast
1 tbsp fish sauce
zest and juice ½ lime (about 1 tbsp)
1 tsp caster sugar
100g bag mixed leaves
large handful coriander, roughly
    chopped
¼ red onion, thinly sliced
½ chilli, deseeded and thinly sliced
¼ cucumber, halved lengthways, sliced

1 Cover the chicken with cold water, bring to the boil, then cook for around 10 minutes. Remove from the pan and cool, then tear into shreds. Stir together the fish sauce, lime zest, juice and sugar until the sugar dissolves.
2 Put the leaves and coriander in a container, then top with the chicken, onion, chilli and cucumber; this will keep in the fridge, covered, overnight.
3 Put the dressing in a separate container and toss through the salad when ready to eat.

PER SERVING 109 kcals, protein 19g, carbs 6g, fat 1g, sat fat none, fibre 1g, sugar 5g, salt 1.6g

Two bean, potato & tuna salad

You'll find soya beans in the vegetable section of the supermarket freezer cabinet.

TAKES 25 MINUTES ● SERVES 4

300g/10oz new potatoes, cut into chunks

175g/6oz green beans, trimmed and halved

175g/6oz frozen soya beans

160g can tuna in spring water, drained well

good handful rocket or watercress leaves

FOR THE DRESSING

2 tsp harissa paste

1 tbsp red wine vinegar

2 tbsp olive oil

1 Put the potatoes in a pan of boiling water, then boil for 6–8 minutes until almost tender. Add both types of beans, then cook for a further 5 minutes until everything is cooked.

2 Meanwhile, make the dressing. Whisk together the harissa and vinegar in a small bowl with a little seasoning. Whisk in the oil until the dressing is thickened. Drain the potatoes and beans well, toss with half of the dressing, then leave to cool.

3 Flake the tuna, then fold into the potatoes. Add the remaining dressing, then gently toss – this will now keep covered in the fridge for up 2 days.

4 When ready to eat, divide among four bowls and serve each portion with a handful of rocket or watercress on top.

PER SERVING 211 kcals, protein 15g, carbs 19g, fat 9g, sat fat 1g, fibre 4g, sugar 2g, salt 0.14g

Cheese & chive coleslaw

Homemade coleslaw makes the perfect accompaniment to a picnic feast and is delicious served with crusty rolls and ham.

TAKES 15 MINUTES ● **SERVES 4–6**

1 white cabbage (about 400g/14 oz)
1 carrot, coarsely grated
1 red onion, halved and thinly sliced
3 tbsp good-quality mayonnaise
3 tbsp low-fat natural yogurt
1 tsp Dijon mustard
20g pack chives, snipped
100g/4oz reduced-fat mature Cheddar, grated

1 Cut the cabbage in half, then cut it into quarters. Remove and discard the core, then thinly shred the leaves. Put into a large mixing bowl. Add the carrot, onion, mayonnaise, yogurt and mustard. Snip in most of the chives.

2 Mix the coleslaw well with your hands, making sure every bit of salad is coated in the dressing. Season, then cover and chill for up to 3 days. Serve sprinkled with the chives and cheese.

PER SERVING (4) 192 kcals, protein 11g, carbs 8g, fat 13g, sat fat 4g, fibre 3g, sugar 8g, salt 0.74g

Make-it-your-own pasta salad

Use this recipe as a base and add chunks of ham, salami or leftover cooked chicken to it, or flake in hot-smoked salmon or smoked mackerel before serving.

TAKES 20 MINUTES • SERVES 4

250g/9oz pasta shapes
140g/5oz frozen peas
pack parsley, chopped
small pack chives, snipped
zest and juice 1 lemon
2 tbsp olive oil
ham, salami or cooked chicken (as
    you choose)

1 Cook the pasta according to the pack instructions, adding the peas for the final 2 minutes of cooking time. Drain, rinse with cold water to cool, then drain again. Tip into a bowl with the chopped herbs, lemon zest and juice, olive oil and plenty of seasoning, and mix well.

2 Cover and chill for up to 3 days, spooning out portions and adding extra ingredients as and when you want.

PER SERVING 292 kcals, protein 10g, carbs 51g, fat 7g, sat fat 1g, fibre 4g, sugar 3g, salt 0.02g

Coconut-crusted lime chicken

Delicious hot with rice or cold with chutney, or served alongside a salad.

TAKES 40 MINUTES • SERVES 4

8 boneless skinless chicken thighs
zest and juice 2 limes, plus extra
    wedges to squeeze
2 tsp medium curry powder or garam
    masala
1 tsp chilli powder (optional)
50g/2oz desiccated coconut
1 tbsp vegetable oil
mango chutney and rice or crisp salad,
    to serve

1 Heat oven to 200C/180C fan/gas 6. Put the chicken in a large bowl with the lime zest and juice, curry powder or garam masala, chilli powder, if using, and some seasoning. Mix well, then toss in the coconut.
2 Put the chicken on a wire rack sitting in a roasting tin, drizzle with the oil, then bake for 25 minutes until cooked through and tender.
3 Serve with mango chutney, lime wedges for squeezing over and rice, if you like, or leave to go cold and keep for up to 2 days and serve with a crisp salad.

PER SERVING 316 kcals, protein 41g, carbs 2g, fat 16g, sat fat 9g, fibre 2g, sugar 1g, salt 0.49g

Feta & sweetcorn samosas

Samosas freeze really well. This quantity makes 12 substantial ones, or you can try your hand at making smaller ones.

❄ ● **TAKES 50 MINUTES** ● **MAKES 14**

350g/12oz frozen sweetcorn
2 tbsp vegetable oil
2 tsp cumin seeds
1 large red onion, finely diced
2 tsp garam masala
200g/7oz feta cheese
juice 1 lime
6 sheets filo pastry
3 tbsp vegetable oil
2 tsp cornflour

1 Cook the sweetcorn in boiling water for about 3 minutes and drain. Heat the oil in a wok or large pan and toss in the cumin seeds. Swirl them around for 30 seconds then add the onion and cook until softened. Stir in the corn, garam masala, feta and lime juice, and continue frying for 1 minute. Leave to cool.

2 Lay out a sheet of filo and cut it lengthways into half. Brush with oil and spoon 2 tablespoons of mix on to the top of each strip and fold each over into a triangle. Keep folding until each strip of filo is used up. Make a thin paste with cornflour mixed with water and brush over the edges to seal. You can now freeze the samosas for 1 month.

3 To cook, heat oven to 200C/180C fan/gas 6. Put the samosas on a baking sheet and brush the tops with oil. Bake for 15 minutes (25–30 minutes from frozen) until golden and crisp and hot in the middle. Serve immediately.

PER SAMOSA 131 kcals, protein 4g, carbs 12g, fat 8g, sat fat 3g, fibre 1g, sugar 2g, salt 0.60g

Spanish spinach omelette

A large omelette makes a great family standby as it keeps well at room temperature or in the fridge, so everyone can cut portions as they come and go.

TAKES 15 MINUTES • SERVES 8

400g bag spinach leaves
3 tbsp olive oil
1 large onion, finely sliced
2 large potatoes, peeled and finely
    sliced
10 eggs

1 Tip the spinach into a large colander and bring a kettle of water to the boil. Slowly pour the water over the spinach until wilted, then cool under cold water. Squeeze all the liquid out of the spinach.

2 Heat grill to high. Heat the oil in a non-stick frying pan and gently cook the onion and potatoes for about 10 minutes until the potatoes are soft.

3 Meanwhile, beat the eggs in a large bowl and season. Stir the spinach into the potatoes, then pour in the eggs and cook, stirring occasionally, until nearly set, then flash the omelette under the grill to set the top.

4 Ease the omelette on to a plate, then flip over back into the pan. Finish cooking the omelette on the underside and turn out on to a board and leave to cool. The omelette can stay at room temperature overnight or will keep in the fridge for up to 2 days. Eat cut into wedges and enjoy cold or reheat in the microwave.

PER SERVING 209 kcals, protein 12g, carbs 11g, fat 13g, sat fat 3g, fibre 2g, sugar 2g, salt 0.46g

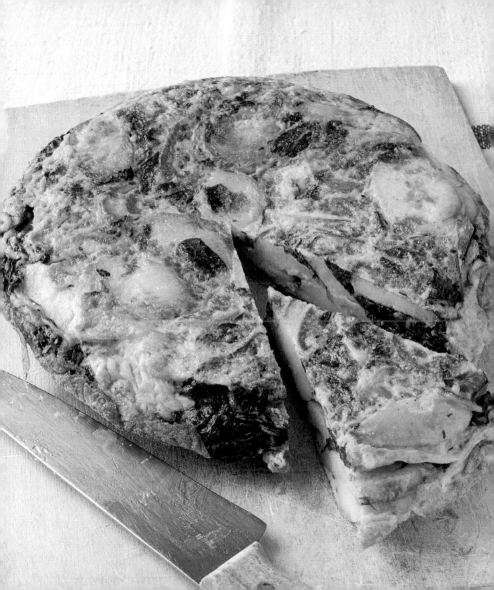

Smoked mackerel, orange & couscous salad

Sliced oranges make a refreshing addition to this substantial salad, which is also great for a lunch box.

TAKES 15 MINUTES • SERVES 4

200g/7oz couscous (use wholemeal
   if you can get it)
3 oranges, 2 peeled and thinly sliced,
   1 juiced
3 tbsp red wine vinegar
1 tsp sugar
3 tbsp olive oil
1 red onion, finely chopped
240g pack peppered mackerel fillets,
   flaked into large chunks
100g bag watercress, roughly chopped

1 Pour 250ml/9fl oz boiling water over the couscous in a large bowl, cover and leave for 10 minutes, then fluff up with a fork.

2 Meanwhile, make the dressing. Mix the orange juice, vinegar, sugar and oil with some seasoning. Mix through the couscous with all the remaining ingredients except the watercress. The salad will now keep covered in the fridge for up to 2 days. Toss the watercress through the couscous just before serving.

PER SERVING 456 kcals, protein 16g, carbs 38g, fat 27g, sat fat 5g, fibre 2g, sugar 12g, salt 1.17g

Mini carrot muffins

These will keep for a couple of days so a great one to make on a Sunday for you to add to the family lunchboxes at the start of the week.

❄ ● **TAKES 25 MINUTES** ● **MAKES 18**

100g/4oz self-raising flour
½ tsp ground mixed spice
100g/4oz golden caster sugar
75ml/2½fl oz sunflower oil
50ml/2fl oz skimmed milk
1 medium egg, lightly beaten
125g/5oz carrots, peeled and grated

1 Heat oven to 190C/170C fan/gas 5. Line two mini muffin trays with 18 muffin cases. Put the flour, mixed spice and sugar into a bowl. Add the oil, milk and egg, then the carrots. Stir to combine.
2 Put a heaped teaspoon of the mixture into each muffin case, then bake for 12 minutes until risen. Cool. Will keep for up to 5 days in an airtight container or can be frozen for up to 3 months.

PER MUFFIN 82 kcals, protein 1g, carbs 11g, fat 4g, sat fat 2g, fibre none, sugar 7g, salt 0.07g

Wholemeal spinach & potato pies

A healthier, vegetarian take on the good old pasty; the robust wholemeal pastry means they keep and freeze well, too.

❄ ● **TAKES 1 HOUR 10 MINUTES**
● **MAKES 8**

140g/5oz plain wholemeal flour
140g/5oz plain white flour, plus extra for dusting
85g/3oz cold butter, diced
85g/3oz shredded vegetable suet
100ml/3½fl oz milk (you may not need all of it)
1 egg, beaten, for glazing

FOR THE FILLING

1 small baking potato, peeled and cut into small chunks
200g/7oz spinach leaves
150ml pot single cream
1 egg, beaten
100g/4oz Cheddar, grated
grated fresh nutmeg

1 Rub the flours together with the butter and suet to breadcrumbs, then add as much of the milk as needed to make the pastry come together. Knead until soft. Press into a round, then chill for 1 hour.

2 Boil the potatoes until cooked, then drain. Tip the spinach into a colander, pour over boiling water, then squeeze dry. In a bowl, mix the spinach with the potatoes, cream, egg and two-thirds of the cheese. Season, add nutmeg, then set aside. Heat oven to 200C/180C fan/gas 6.

3 Roll the pastry on a floured surface. Cut out eight squares roughly 13cm. Spoon the mix on to each square, then brush the edges with beaten egg. Bring the pastry together, pinching the edges together to seal. They can now be covered and frozen; defrost before cooking.

4 Transfer to a baking sheet. Brush each pie with egg, then top with a large pinch of the remaining grated cheese. Bake for 30 minutes until golden, then cool.

PER PIE 421 kcals, protein 11g, carbs 31g, fat 31g, sat fat 11g, fibre 3g, sugar 2g, salt 0.57g

Chicken & bean enchiladas

Take the stress out of Monday's supper by preparing this on Sunday night using leftover roast chicken from lunch.

TAKES 40 MINUTES ● SERVES 4

1 tbsp vegetable oil
1 red onion, chopped
1 garlic clove, crushed
1 tbsp fajita seasoning
2 × 395g cans kidney beans in chilli sauce
2 roast chicken legs, meat shredded off the bone
195g can sweetcorn, drained
8 flour tortillas
140g/5oz Cheddar, grated

1 Heat the oil in a frying pan and cook the onion and garlic for 5 minutes. Stir in the fajita seasoning and cook for 1 minute more before adding the kidney beans, shredded chicken and sweetcorn.
2 Divide the chicken and bean mixture among the tortillas, sprinkle over half the cheese, then roll up and put in a baking dish. Sprinkle over the remaining cheese and the enchiladas can now be covered and left in the fridge overnight.
3 To cook, heat oven to 180C/160C fan/gas 4 and then bake for 20–25 minutes until golden and bubbling.

PER SERVING 842 kcals, protein 46g, carbs 88g, fat 36g, sat fat 14g, fibre 11g, sugar 16g, salt 4.52g

Leek & goat's cheese tartlets

These clever little tarts can be prepared, frozen, then cooked straight from the freezer – what could be easier on a weeknight?

❄ **UNBAKED** • **TAKES 1 HOUR**
• **SERVES 4**

4 leeks, trimmed, halved and finely
  sliced
large knob butter
2 tbsp thyme leaves plus 4 nice sprigs
375g block puff pastry
4 slices goat's cheese (with a rind)

1 Wash the leeks in a colander but don't dry them as you want a bit of water clinging on. Heat the butter in a wide pan until sizzling, then add the wet leeks and thyme leaves, and season with salt and pepper. Sweat the leeks gently for 20–25 minutes until they have softened but not coloured, adding a little more butter if needed. Set aside to cool.

2 Roll the pastry out to the thickness of a £1 coin. Cut out four saucer-size circles and put on a baking sheet. Spread the leeks over the circles, leaving a border around the edge. Put a slice of goat's cheese in the middle of each tart and top with a thyme sprig. Pinch the pastry edges together to slightly encase the leeks. The tarts can now be covered and chilled for 2 days or frozen for 1 month.

3 To cook, heat oven to 220C/200C fan/gas 7. Put the tarts on a baking sheet then bake for 25 minutes, or about 35 minutes from frozen, until puffed up and golden.

PER SERVING 606 kcals, protein 18g, carbs 32g, fat 46g, sat fat 24g, fibre 4g, sugar 4g, salt 1.82g

Italian-style stuffed aubergines

Longer rather than wider aubergines work best for stuffing and hold their shape when baked.

TAKES 50 MINUTES • SERVES 4

2 aubergines
2 tbsp olive oil, plus extra for drizzling
1 large onion, finely chopped
4 garlic cloves, finely chopped
12 cherry tomatoes, halved
50g/2oz pitted green olives, chopped
handful basil leaves, chopped
125g ball vegetarian mozzarella, torn
  into bite-size pieces
handful fresh white breadcrumbs

1 Heat oven to 220C/200C fan/gas 7. Slice the aubergines in half lengthways, leaving the stem intact. Using a small knife, cut a border inside each aubergine about 0.5–1cm/¼–½in thick. Using a teaspoon, scoop out the aubergine flesh, so that you have four shells. Brush these with a little of the oil, season and put in a baking dish. Cover and bake for 20 minutes. Chop the flesh and set aside.
2 Add the remaining oil to a non-stick frying pan. Tip in the onion and cook until soft. Add the aubergine flesh and cook through. Tip in the garlic and tomatoes, and cook for 3 minutes. Stir in the olives, basil, mozzarella and some seasoning. When the shells are tender, remove from the oven and fill with the stuffing. They can now be chilled for up to 2 days.
3 To finish, heat oven to 200C/180C fan/gas 6. Sprinkle with breadcrumbs and drizzle with a little more oil. Bake for 20–25 minutes and serve with a salad.

PER SERVING 266 kcals, protein 9g, carbs 14g, fat 20g, sat fat 6g, fibre 5g, sugar 7g, salt 1.17g

Spicy turkey & pepper bake

This tasty mash-topped bake is lighter, quicker and healthier than a classic shepherd's or cottage pie.

❄ ● **TAKES 1 HOUR** ● **SERVES 4**

1kg/2lb 4oz potatoes, peeled and
  chopped
25g/1oz butter
300g/10oz frozen sliced mixed peppers
1 onion, chopped
500g pack minced turkey
1 red chilli, deseeded and chopped
1 tbsp smoked paprika
200ml/7fl oz hot chicken stock

1 Cook the potatoes in a large pan of salted water for 12–15 minutes or until tender. Drain well, then return to the pan and allow to steam for 3 minutes. Add some seasoning and the butter, then roughly mash with a fork and set aside until later.

2 Meanwhile, cook the peppers and onion in a large pan for 5 minutes – the water in the peppers should stop them sticking. Stir in the turkey mince, chilli and paprika, and cook until browned. Pour in the stock, then bubble for 10 minutes until thickened.

3 Transfer the turkey mince mix to an ovenproof dish and top with the mash. The bake can now be chilled for up to 2 days or frozen for 3 months.

4 To cook, heat oven to 200C/180C fan/ gas 6 and bake for about 40 minutes or until golden and bubbling (defrost frozen bakes thoroughly before cooking).

PER SERVING 410 kcals, protein 37g, carbs 50g, fat 8g, sat fat 4g, fibre 5g, sugar 7g, salt 0.45g

Sausage & bean casserole

This kid-friendly combination of sausages and beans is all cooked in one pan to save on washing up.

❄ • **TAKES 1 HOUR** • **SERVES 4**

1 tbsp vegetable oil
8 pork sausages
2 celery sticks, chopped
2 carrots, chopped
1 onion, chopped
1 tbsp tomato purée
400g can butter beans
400g can baked beans in tomato sauce
½ small bunch thyme
200ml/7fl oz hot chicken or veg stock
2 slices white bread, whizzed to
    crumbs

1 Heat half the oil in a large casserole dish, then brown the sausages all over. Remove from the dish and set aside. Add the remaining oil, tip the veg into the dish and fry for 10 minutes. Stir in the tomato purée and cook for 1 minute more.

2 Return the sausages to the dish with the beans, thyme and some seasoning, then pour in the stock and bring to a simmer. Remove from the heat. The sausages can now be cooled and chilled for up to 2 days or frozen for 3 months – defrost completely before reheating.

3 To finish, heat oven to 200C/180C fan/ gas 6 and tip the stew back into the casserole dish. Sprinkle over the breadcrumbs, then bake in the oven for 25–30 minutes until the crumbs are golden and the stew is bubbling.

PER SERVING 580 kcals, protein 25g, carbs 50g, fat 33g, sat fat 10g, fibre 10g, sugar 16g, salt 3.85g

Cauliflower & macaroni cheese

To add a twist you can replace the cauliflower with broccoli or use half and half of the two.

❄ ● **TAKES 1 HOUR** ● **SERVES 4**

250g/9oz macaroni
1 head cauliflower, broken into pieces
25g/1oz butter
2 tbsp plain flour
2 tsp English mustard powder
450ml/16fl oz milk
100g/4oz Cheddar, grated

1 Cook the macaroni according to the pack instructions, adding the cauliflower for the final 4 minutes.
2 Melt the butter in a pan, then stir in the flour and mustard powder, and cook for 2 minutes. Gradually add the milk, stirring all the time to get a smooth sauce. Add three-quarters of the cheese and some seasoning to the sauce.
3 Drain the macaroni and cauliflower, and stir into the cheese sauce. Transfer to an ovenproof dish, then sprinkle over the remaining cheese. The dish can now be cooled and chilled and kept for 2 days or frozen for 3 months. Defrost completely before reheating.
4 If cooking while still warm, flash under a hot grill until golden and bubbling. If cooking from cold, heat oven to 200C/180C fan/gas 6 and bake for 30 minutes.

PER SERVING 446 kcals, protein 19g, carbs 57g, fat 17g, sat fat 10g, fibre 2g, sugar 7g, salt 0.68g

Pan-fried chicken with tomato & olive sauce

A recipe for late summer that takes advantage of juicy, ripe home-grown tomatoes and basil.

❄ ● TAKES 30 MINUTES ● SERVES 2

2 tbsp olive oil
2 boneless skinless chicken breasts
1 small onion, halved and very thinly
  sliced
2 garlic cloves, sliced
400g/14oz ripe tomatoes, finely
  chopped
1 tbsp balsamic vinegar
6 pimiento-stuffed green olives, thickly
  sliced
300ml/½ pint chicken stock
generous handful basil leaves

1 Heat the oil in a large non-stick frying pan, then season the chicken and fry, flattest-side down, for 4–5 minutes. Turn the chicken over, add the onion and cook for 4–5 minutes more. Lift the chicken from the pan and set aside. Add the garlic to the pan, then continue cooking until the onions are soft.

2 Tip in the tomatoes with the balsamic vinegar, olives, stock and some seasoning, then simmer, stirring frequently, for 7–8 minutes until pulpy. Return the chicken and any juices to the pan and gently simmer, covered, for 5 minutes more, to cook the chicken through.

3 The chicken can now be cooled and chilled for 2 days or frozen for 2 months then defrosted completely. Reheat gently in a pan or in a microwave and stir through half the basil. Serve scattered with the rest of the basil.

PER SERVING 353 kcals, protein 41g, carbs 11g, fat 17g, sat fat 3g, fibre 4g, sugar 9g, salt 2.15g

Butternut squash salad

A delicious, superhealthy vegetarian main-meal salad that can be made and eaten over a couple of days.

TAKES 1 HOUR • SERVES 4

1 butternut squash, peeled, deseeded
   and diced
2 tbsp olive oil
50g/2oz wild and brown rice
50g/2oz Puy lentils
1 head broccoli, cut into florets
50g/4oz dried cranberries
25g/1oz pumpkin seeds
juice 1 lemon

1 Heat oven to 200C/180C fan/gas 6. Spread the squash over a large baking sheet, drizzle over half the oil and bake for 30 minutes or until tender.

2 Meanwhile, cook the rice and lentils in boiling salted water for 20 minutes, adding the broccoli for the final 4 minutes of cooking. Drain well, then stir in the cranberries and pumpkin seeds with some seasoning. Add the squash, pour over the rest of the olive oil and the lemon juice. This salad can now be kept in the fridge for up to 2 days – just remove it from the fridge about an hour before eating to take the chill off it.

PER SERVING 266 kcals, protein 12g, carbs 43g, fat 7g, sat fat 1g, fibre 7g, sugar 18g, salt 0.05g

One-pan prawn & tomato curry

Remember, if you want to freeze this tasty one-pan curry you must use fresh prawns not frozen.

❄ ● **TAKES 30 MINUTES** ● **SERVES 4**

2 tbsp sunflower oil
1 large onion, chopped
large piece ginger, crushed
4 garlic cloves, crushed
½ red chilli, finely chopped
1 tsp golden caster sugar
1 tsp black mustard seeds
1 tsp ground cumin
1 tsp ground coriander
1 tsp ground turmeric
1 tbsp garam masala
2 tsp malt vinegar
400g can chopped tomatoes
400g/14oz raw peeled king prawns
small bunch coriander, chopped

1 Heat the oil in a deep-sided frying pan and cook the onion for 8–10 minutes until it starts to turn golden. Add the ginger, garlic and chilli, and cook for 1–2 minutes. Stir in the sugar and spices for 1 minute, then splash in the vinegar and tomatoes. Season with salt and simmer for 5 minutes, stirring, until the sauce thickens.

2 Stir in the prawns, reduce the heat and cook for 8–10 minutes until cooked through – if the sauce gets really thick, add a splash of water. The curry can now be cooled and chilled for 24 hours or frozen for a month. Defrost completely in the fridge before reheating.

3 Reheat gently in a pan, adding a splash more water if needed, and stir though most of the coriander. Serve straight from the dish scattered with the remaining coriander.

PER SERVING 217 kcals, protein 22g, carbs 16g, fat 8g, sat fat 1g, fibre 3g, sugar 9g, salt 0.66g

Italian sausage & pasta pot

This is a fantastic one-pot meal packed with flavour, as the stock is enriched with all the ingredients cooked in it.

TAKES 35 MINUTES • SERVES 4

1 tbsp olive oil
8 Italian sausages
2.8 litres/5 pints hot chicken stock
400g/14oz penne
2 carrots, thinly sliced
2 onions, thinly sliced
3 celery sticks, thinly sliced
140g/5oz green beans, cut into
   5cm/2in lengths
handful flat-leaf parsley, chopped

1 Heat the oil in a large pan and fry the sausages until brown all over. Pour in the hot chicken stock and simmer with a lid on for 10 minutes.

2 Add the pasta to the pan, mix well and bring to the boil. Stir in the carrots and onions, cook for 5 minutes, then add the celery and beans, and cook for a further 4 minutes. Check that the pasta is cooked, if not, cook for a few minutes longer. Finally, stir in the chopped parsley and season. The dish can now be cooled and kept in the fridge overnight then reheated, gently adding a splash more stock if needed. Serve in bowls scattered with parsley

PER SERVING 772 kcals, protein 53g, carbs 90g, fat 25g, sat fat 8g, fibre 9g, sugar 11g, salt 3g

Pumpkin curry with chickpeas

A stand-alone vegan main course that also makes a complex side dish to serve with spiced roast meat or fish.

❄ ● **TAKES 40 MINUTES** ● **SERVES 4**

1 tbsp sunflower oil
3 tbsp vegetarian Thai yellow curry
  paste
2 onions, finely chopped
3 large lemongrass stalks, bashed with
  the back of a knife
6 cardamom pods
1 tbsp mustard seed
1 piece pumpkin or 1 small squash
  (about 1kg/2lb 4oz)
250ml/9fl oz vegetable stock
400ml can reduced-fat coconut milk
400g can chickpeas, drained and rinsed
2 limes
large handful mint leaves

1 Heat the oil in a shallow pan, then gently fry the curry paste with the onions, lemongrass, cardamom and mustard seed for 2–3 minutes until fragrant. Stir the pumpkin or squash into the pan and coat in the paste, then pour in the stock and coconut milk. Bring everything to a simmer, add the chickpeas, then cook for about 10 minutes until the pumpkin is tender. The curry can now be cooled and kept for 2 days in the fridge or frozen for up to 1 month. Defrost completely before reheating.
2 Reheat thoroughly and squeeze the juice of one lime into the curry, then cut the other lime into wedges to serve alongside. Just before serving, tear over the mint leaves, then bring to the table with the lime wedges.

PER SERVING 293 kcals, protein 9g, carbs 26g, fat 18g, sat fat 10g, fibre 7g, sugar 10g, salt 1.32g

Smoked trout fish cakes with mushy peas

Using already cooked smoked trout takes some of the hassle out of making fish cakes and adds to the flavour.

❄ • **TAKES 45 MINUTES** • **SERVES 4**

600g/1lb 5oz potatoes, diced
2 tbsp hot horseradish sauce
200g/7oz smoked trout fillets, flaked
zest and juice 1 lemon, plus extra
   lemon wedges to squeeze
25g/1oz plain flour
400g/14oz frozen peas
100ml/3½fl oz hot vegetable stock
1 tbsp vegetable oil

1 Cook the potatoes in boiling salted water until tender. Drain really well, then return to the pan and steam-dry for a few minutes. Remove from the heat, add the horseradish, then mash together.
2 Stir in the trout, zest and half the juice with some seasoning. Make eight patties, dust lightly with flour, then chill for up to 2 days or freeze for 1 month. Defrost completely in the fridge before cooking.
3 Put the peas in a pan with the stock and bring to the boil, reduce the heat and cook for 3 minutes. Transfer to a food processor and whizz for 30 seconds to a crush. Tip them back into the pan, add the remaining lemon juice and some seasoning. Cool and chill for up to 2 days.
4 Heat the oil in a frying pan until hot, cook the fish cakes for 3–4 minutes on each side until golden and crisp – you may have to do this in batches. Serve with reheated mushy peas and some extra lemon wedges on the side.

PER SERVING 329 kcals, protein 20g, carbs 42g, fat 10g, sat fat 2g, fibre 8g, sugar 5g, salt 1.28g

Crumbly chicken & mixed vegetable pie

This veg-packed pie makes a whole new meal from leftover roast chicken.

❄ • TAKES 1¼ HOURS • SERVES 4

50g/2oz butter

1 onion, very finely chopped

100g/4oz button mushrooms, sliced

50g/2oz plain flour, plus extra for dusting

400ml/14fl oz milk, warmed

400ml/14fl oz chicken stock

pinch nutmeg

pinch mustard powder

1 bay leaf

250g/9oz cooked chicken, cut into chunks

200g/7oz mix sweetcorn, peas, chopped peppers, broccoli, carrots or other veg

250g/9oz shortcrust pastry

1 egg, beaten, or milk, for glazing

1 Melt the butter in a pan over a medium heat. Add the onion and cook, stirring occasionally, for 5 minutes then add the mushrooms. When almost cooked, add the flour to the pan and stir to make a thick paste, then cook over a low heat for 2 minutes. Slowly add the warm milk to the pan while stirring. Stir in the stock, season with salt, pepper, nutmeg and mustard powder. Add the bay leaf and bring to the boil, stirring all the time, until thickened. Add the chicken and veg, and pour into the pie dish. Leave to cool. This can be made a day ahead or frozen for a month – defrost before you continue.

2 Roll the pastry out and lift it carefully over the pie dish. Trim off any excess. Press the outside edge of the pastry with your fingers to make a nice pattern.

3 Heat oven to 200C/180C fan/gas 6. Brush the top of the pie with beaten egg or milk. Make a small hole in the centre of the pastry top and put the pie in the oven for 25 minutes, until golden brown.

PER SERVING 583 kcals, protein 27g, carbs 48g, fat 33g, sat fat 15g, fibre 3g, sugar 9g, salt 2.11g

Vegetable & bean chilli

A versatile vegetarian chilli that can be served with rice, used as a baked potato topping or to fill a tortilla wrap.

TAKES 45 MINUTES • SERVES 4

1 tbsp olive oil
1 garlic clove, finely chopped
thumb-size piece ginger, finely chopped
1 large onion, chopped
2 courgettes, diced
1 red pepper, deseeded and chopped
1 yellow pepper, deseeded and
    chopped
1 tbsp chilli powder
100g/4oz red lentils, rinsed and drained
1 tbsp tomato purée
2 × 400g cans chopped tomatoes
195g can sweetcorn, drained
420g can butter beans, drained
    and rinsed
400g can kidney beans in water,
    drained and rinsed

1 Heat the oil in a large pan. Cook the garlic, ginger, onion, courgettes and peppers for about 5 minutes until starting to soften. Add the chilli powder and cook for 1 minute more.
2 Stir in the lentils, tomato purée, tomatoes and 250ml/9fl oz water. Bring to the boil and cook for 15–20 minutes.
3 Add the sweetcorn and beans, and cook for a further 10 minutes. Enjoy straight away or leave to cool then keep in the fridge for up to 3 days. Reheat gently in a pan or in the microwave.

PER SERVING 361 kcals, protein 21g, carbs 61g, fat 6g, sat fat 10g, fibre 13g, sugar 21g, salt 1.34g

Moroccan-style chicken stew

This one-pan supper uses sliced chicken breasts, but you could use chicken thighs –
they would just need to be cooked for longer.

❄ ● **TAKES 30 MINUTES** ● **SERVES 4**

1 tbsp olive oil
1 onion, chopped
1 garlic clove, crushed
1 tbsp ras-el-hanout or Moroccan
  spice mix
4 boneless skinless chicken breasts,
  sliced
300ml/½ pint chicken stock
400g can chickpeas, drained and rinsed
12 dried apricots, sliced
small bunch coriander, chopped

1 Heat the oil in a large shallow pan, then cook the onion for 3 minutes. Add the garlic and spices, and cook for a further minute.

2 Tip in the chicken and cook for 3 minutes, then pour in the chicken stock, chickpeas and apricots. Simmer for 5 minutes or until the chicken is cooked through. The stew can now be cooled and chilled, and reheated gently in a pan or in the microwave. The stew can also be frozen for up to 3 months – defrost completely before reheating.

3 Just before serving, stir through the coriander and eat with couscous and a green salad, if you like.

PER SERVING 309 kcals, protein 40g, carbs 24g, fat 6g, sat fat 1g, fibre 5g, sugar 13g, salt 0.66g

Salmon, squash & prawn laksa

Laksa paste is available from specialist oriental supermarkets, or you can use the more readily available Thai red curry paste instead.

❄ ● TAKES 40 MINUTES ● SERVES 6

185g jar laksa paste
1 small butternut squash (about
    600g/1lb 5oz once peeled), peeled,
    deseeded and cut into chunks
400ml can coconut milk
600ml/1 pint chicken stock
140g/5oz medium rice noodles, soaked
    in boiling water and drained
300g pack beansprouts
400g/14oz skinless salmon fillet, cut
    into large chunks
200g/7oz tail-on prawns
bunch spring onions, sliced
small bunch coriander leaves,
    to sprinkle
lime wedges, to squeeze

1 Heat the paste in a large pan and fry the squash for a few minutes until well coated in the paste. Pour in the coconut milk and stock, and simmer for about 10 minutes. The squash should still have a bite to it. Add the drained noodles and beansprouts.

2 To freeze, turn off the heat straight away and leave to cool, then transfer to a suitable container and freeze for up to 2 months. If you're making this to eat now, add the salmon and prawns, and cook for 4–5 minutes until the fish is cooked through.

3 If frozen, defrost overnight in the fridge, then return to a large pan. Add the salmon and prawns, cover, bring to the boil and simmer until the fish is cooked – it should only take 1–2 minutes. Stir through the spring onions, then sprinkle with the coriander and serve with some lime wedges.

PER SERVING 445 kcals, protein 29g, carbs 34g, fat 23g, sat fat 11g, fibre 3g, sugar 9g, salt 1.18g

Thai green chicken soup

This recipe makes a large amount, but it's perfect for freezing in portions in small bags. Lay them flat in the freezer so the soup will thaw more quickly when removed.

❄ • **TAKES 1 HOUR** • **SERVES 8**

2 tbsp sunflower oil
1 onion, finely chopped
500g pack skinless chicken thigh fillets, finely chopped
4 garlic cloves, finely sliced
285g jar Thai green curry paste
400ml can coconut milk
1.75 litres/3 pints chicken stock
5 kaffir lime leaves
2 tbsp fish sauce
1 bunch spring onions, the white sliced on the diagonal and the green finely chopped
280g pack fine green beans, trimmed and halved
150g pack bamboo shoots
juice 2 limes, plus wedges to squeeze
small bunch basil

1 Heat the oil in your largest pan, add the onion and fry for 3 minutes to soften. Add the chicken and garlic, and cook until the chicken changes colour.

2 Add the curry paste, coconut milk, stock, lime leaves and fish sauce, then simmer for 12 minutes. Add the chopped onion tops, green beans and bamboo shoots, and cook for 4–6 minutes, until the beans are just tender.

3 Meanwhile, put the lime juice and basil in a narrow jug and blitz with a hand blender to make a smooth green paste. Pour into the soup with the sliced spring onion and heat through. The soup can now be cooled and frozen. To eat, defrost, if necessary, and reheat until piping hot. Serve with lime wedges for a light lunch or as a make-ahead starter for supper.

PER SERVING 262 kcals, protein 23g, carbs 8g, fat 16g, sat fat 8g, fibre 3g, sugar 4g, salt 2.38g

Bake-from-the-freezer pizzas

Make sure you dry the mozzarella well with kitchen paper – this will help to keep the pizza base really crisp.

❄ • **TAKES 45 MINUTES, PLUS RISING**
• **MAKES 6**

500g pack bread mix or pizza base mix
oil, for greasing
a little plain flour, for rolling
6 tbsp tomato pasta sauce or passata
small bunch basil leaves, shredded
18 cherry tomatoes, halved
250g ball mozzarella
25g/1oz Parmesan, grated

1 Make up the bread or pizza mix according to the pack instructions, and put in an oiled bowl to rise for 1 hour.
2 Knock back in the bowl by squashing all the air out of the dough with your fist. Divide the dough into six and roll each one on a lightly floured surface to a circle about 18cm in diameter. Put the dough you're not using under a damp tea towel or oiled cling film to stop it drying out.
3 Put the pizza bases on large oiled baking sheets – you may need two or three. Spread 1 tablespoon of the sauce or passata on each base, then scatter on the basil, tomatoes, mozzarella and Parmesan (or whatever you fancy). You can freeze the pizzas now, if you like, on the baking sheet, wrapped in cling film.
4 To cook from frozen, remove the cling film and heat oven to 220C/200C fan/ gas 7. Bake for 10–14 minutes until crisp and golden.

PER PIZZA 380 kcals, protein 18g, carbs 51g, fat 13g, sat fat 7g, fibre 5g, sugar 4g, salt 2.53g

Mushroom, shallot & squash pie

A full-flavoured vegetarian pie that everyone will be happy to eat.

❄ ● TAKES 3 HOURS ● SERVES 6

600g/1lb 5oz shallots, halved
1 tbsp olive oil
100g/4oz butter
1 butternut squash, peeled, deseeded
  and diced
2 garlic cloves, finely chopped
2 tsp finely chopped rosemary leaves
2 tsp finely chopped sage leaves
250g/9oz fresh mushrooms (such as
  Portobello or chestnut), sliced
25g/1oz dried porcini mushrooms,
  soaked in 250ml/9fl oz boiling water
50g/2oz plain flour, plus a little extra
  for dusting
500ml/18fl oz vegetable stock
500g pack puff pastry
1 egg, beaten

1 Soften the shallots in the olive oil and a third of the butter. Add the squash and cook until softening, then add the garlic and herbs, and cook for 2 minutes more.
2 In another pan, fry the fresh mushrooms in another third of butter. Strain the porcini, reserving the soaking liquid, then roughly chop and add to the cooked mushrooms. Fry for 2 minutes, then remove from the pan and set aside.
3 Melt the remaining butter in the same pan, stir in the flour for 2 minutes, then stir in the stock and mushroom liquid. Bring to the boil, stirring, and cook until thickened. Combine the sauce with all the veg, then transfer to a pie dish. Cool.
4 Roll out the pastry on a floured surface. Cover the pie, trimming the excess pastry, then wrap in cling film. Freeze for up to 2 months. Defrost before cooking.
5 To cook, heat oven to 200C/180C fan/ gas 6, glaze the pastry with egg and bake for 30–40 minutes until golden.

PER SERVING 610 kcals, protein 12g, carbs 51g, fat 42g, sat fat 21g, fibre 7g, sugar 12g, salt 1.32g

Pork goulash with herby dumplings

Goulash makes a great freezer standby – just the job when you're pushed for time but want the comfort of a warming stew.

❄ ● TAKES 2 HOURS ● SERVES 10

2 tbsp olive oil

1.5kg/3lb 5oz pork tenderloin, cut into strips

2 onions, cut into thin wedges

4 garlic cloves, crushed

1–2 tbsp smoked paprika

500ml/18fl oz beef stock

2 × 400g cans chopped tomatoes

1 tbsp sugar

3 red peppers, deseeded and chopped

FOR THE DUMPLINGS

250g/9oz self-raising flour

140g/5oz shredded suet

1½ tsp baking powder

small bunch oregano, most leaves chopped

1 Heat half the oil in a casserole dish and fry the pork for 4–5 minutes until browned. Set aside. Use the remaining oil to fry the onions for 8–10 minutes until soft, then add the garlic and paprika, and cook for 1–2 minutes more. Return the pork to the dish and pour in the stock, tomatoes and sugar. Bring to the boil, then turn down and simmer for around 20–30 minutes until thickened.

2 For the dumplings, combine all the ingredients, apart from the oregano, with enough cold water to make a scone-like dough. Roll into about 30 walnut-size balls. Stir the peppers into the goulash, tuck in the dumplings, cover and cook for 25–30 minutes. Allow to cool and freeze for up to 2 months, or serve with the reserved oregano.

3 If frozen, defrost then reheat in the microwave on Medium for 4–6 minutes (longer for larger servings), or gently on the hob, covered, until piping hot.

PER SERVING 476 kcals, protein 38g, carbs 27g, fat 25g, sat fat 10g, fibre 2g, sugar 5g, salt 0.84g

Bombay potato & spinach pies

These are ideal for a lunch with salad or as part of a buffet and are no hassle to make.

❄ ● **TAKES 1 HOUR 20 MINUTES**
● **MAKES 2 (EACH SERVES 4)**

FOR THE FILLING

1.25kg/2lb 12oz large waxy potatoes such as Charlotte, halved
85g/3oz butter
2 onions, chopped
1 tbsp cumin seeds
1 tbsp black mustard seeds
2 tbsp finely chopped ginger
2 red chillies, halved, deseeded and sliced
3 tbsp Korma curry paste
400g bag spinach leaves
4 tomatoes, chopped
small bunch coriander, chopped

FOR THE PASTRY

270g pack filo pastry (6 large sheets)
50g/2oz butter, melted
1 tsp black mustard seeds

1 Boil the potatoes until tender. Drain. Melt the butter then fry the onions. Add the cumin, mustard, ginger and chillies, and fry until soft. Stir in the curry paste.
2 Cook the spinach in a microwave, drain then chop. Stir the potatoes into the spice mixture. Crush them lightly. Add the spinach, tomatoes and coriander.
3 Brush two 20cm-round loose-bottomed sandwich tins with butter. Brush a sheet of pastry and lay it across a tin so that it hangs over the side. Do the same with another sheet of pastry so the two form a cross. Butter and fold a final sheet in half and lay it in the base of the tin. Repeat with the other tin.
4 Spoon the filling into the tins and fold up the overhanging pastry to cover. Brush with the remaining butter and sprinkle with seeds. The pies can now be frozen for 3 months. To cook, defrost then heat oven to 190C/170C fan/gas 5 and bake for 35 minutes until golden and crisp.

PER SERVING 386 kcals, protein 9g, carbs 51g, fat 18g, sat fat 9g, fibre 5g, sugar 6g, salt 0.87g

Golden veggie shepherd's pie

Make two pies then eat one now and freeze one for later. If time is against you,
swap dried lentils for canned ones.

❄ • **TAKES 2 HOURS** • **SERVES 10**

FOR THE LENTIL SAUCE

50g/2oz butter

2 onions, chopped

4 carrots, diced

1 head celery, chopped

4 garlic cloves, finely chopped

200g pack chestnut mushrooms, sliced

2 bay leaves

1 tbsp dried thyme

500g pack dried green lentils (or use
    3 × 400g cans lentils, drained and
    rinsed)

100ml/3½fl oz red wine (optional)

1.7 litres/3 pints vegetable stock

3 tbsp tomato purée

FOR THE TOPPING

2kg/4lb 8oz floury potatoes

85g/3oz butter

100ml/3½fl oz milk

50g/2oz Cheddar, grated

1 To make the sauce, heat the butter in a pan, then gently fry the onions, carrots, celery and garlic for 15 minutes until soft and golden. Turn up the heat, add the mushrooms, then cook for 4 minutes more. Stir in the herbs, then add the lentils. Pour over the wine, if using, and stock – do not season with salt at this stage. Simmer for 40–50 minutes until the lentils are very soft (if you are using canned lentils, simmer for 10 minutes). Now season to taste, take off the heat, then stir in the purée.

2 While the lentils are cooking, boil the potatoes until tender. Drain well and mash with the butter and milk. Season.

3 To assemble the pies, divide the lentil mixture between two baking dishes, then top with mash. Scatter over the cheese and freeze for up to 2 months or, if eating that day, heat oven to 190C/170C fan/gas 5, then bake for 30 minutes until the topping is golden.

PER SERVING 449 kcals, protein 19g, carbs 68g, fat 13g, sat fat 7g, fibre 10g, sugar 9g, salt 0.59g

Portuguese braised steak & onions

In Portugal, this braise would be served with fried potatoes or rice (or sometimes both), but it goes just as well with a pillow of buttery mash.

❄ • **TAKES 2½ HOURS** • **SERVES 4**

2 tbsp olive oil
4 braising steaks (about 200g/7oz each)
4 tbsp red wine vinegar
3 onions, finely sliced
3 garlic cloves, finely chopped
½ tsp paprika
100ml/3½fl oz red wine
400g can chopped tomatoes
1 tsp tomato purée
2 bay leaves
chopped coriander, to garnish

1 Heat oven to 140C/120C fan/gas 1. Heat half the oil in a shallow casserole dish. Brown the steaks well on each side, then remove from the pan. Splash the vinegar into the pan then let it bubble and almost evaporate. Add the rest of the olive oil and the onions, and gently fry on a medium heat for 10–15 minutes until softened and starting to colour.

2 Once the onions have softened, stir in the garlic and the paprika. Cook for 1 minute more, tip in the red wine and chopped tomatoes, then stir through the tomato purée and bay leaves. Season, pop the steaks back into the pan, then cover and put in the oven for 2 hours, stirring halfway through and adding a splash of water if needed. Cook until the meat is very tender.

3 The stew can now be cooled and chilled for 2 days or frozen for up to 3 months. Defrost before reheating until piping hot. To serve, scatter with coriander.

PER SERVING 430 kcals, protein 44g, carbs 11g, fat 23g, sat fat 8g, fibre 2g, sugar 8g, salt 0.46g

Fuss-free lasagne

Layering lasagne is a great job for kids as it follows an easy pattern. Uncooked, these can be chilled for a day or frozen for up to 3 months. Defrost before cooking.

❄ • **TAKES 2½ HOURS** • **MAKES 2 LASAGNES (EACH SERVES ABOUT 5)**

250g mozzarella, drained and grated
18–20 no-cook lasagne sheets
85g/3oz block Parmesan, grated

FOR THE MEAT SAUCE

3 tbsp olive oil
4 onions, finely chopped
8 garlic cloves, crushed
1 tbsp dried mixed herbs
2 bay leaves
1kg/2lb 4oz minced beef
4 × 400g cans chopped tomatoes

FOR THE WHITE SAUCE

200g/7oz butter
140g/5oz flour
1.7 litres/3 pints milk

1 Heat the oil for the meat sauce in a large pan and gently cook the onions for 10 minutes. Add the garlic and herbs, then cook for 2 minutes more. Heat a frying pan. Brown the beef in batches, then add to the onions. Add the tomatoes, season and gently cook for 30 minutes.

2 For the white sauce, tip everything into a pan, season, then bring to a simmer, whisking continuously. Simmer for 5 minutes, whisking, until smooth and thickened, then remove from the heat.

3 Put a thin layer of meat sauce in two ovenproof baking dishes, drizzle with a little white sauce and scatter with a little mozzarella. Cover with lasagne sheets, then top with more of both sauces, more mozzarella and more lasagne sheets. Repeat once more, then top with white sauce and scatter over some Parmesan. Chill or freeze until ready to cook.

4 To cook, heat oven to 200C/180C fan/ gas 6. Cook for 35–40 minutes.

PER SERVING 847 kcals, protein 43g, carbs 65g, fat 48g, sat fat 25g, fibre 5g, sugar 17g, salt 1.58g

Cheese & tomato pasta bakes

This sort of family meal is well worth making in bulk, so you can eat one now and freeze the rest for another day.

❄ ● **TAKES 1½ HOURS** ● **SERVES 12**

3 tbsp olive oil

1 bag small mixed peppers (about 7 peppers), deseeded and cut into large chunks

6 garlic cloves, chopped

500g pack large button mushrooms, quartered

1 litre carton passata

450ml/16fl oz vegetable stock

2 tsp dried oregano

290g jar pitted Kalamata olives, drained

500g/1lb 2oz large courgettes, halved lengthways and thickly sliced

500g pack dried penne

FOR THE CHEESE SAUCE AND TOPPING

1.5 litres/2¾ pints milk

140g/5oz butter

140g/5oz plain flour

300g/10oz mature Cheddar, grated

85g/3oz hunk old bread, torn into small pieces

1 Heat the oil in a wide pan, then stir-fry the peppers for 5 minutes. Add the garlic and mushrooms, and cook for 5 minutes.
2 Pour in the passata and stock, then stir in the oregano, olives and courgettes with plenty of black pepper. Simmer, stirring frequently, for 10–15 minutes until the veg is just tender and the sauce has reduced a little. Meanwhile, cook the pasta according to the pack instructions.
3 For the cheese sauce, pour the milk into a large pan and add the butter and flour. Heat, whisking all the time until smooth and thick. Stir in half the cheese and allow it to melt into the sauce.
4 Drain the pasta and add to the tomato mixture. Pile into two or three baking dishes, pack down well, then pour over the cheese sauce. Scatter with the remaining cheese and the bread pieces. It can now be frozen for up to 3 months.
5 To serve, bake at 200C/180C fan/ gas 6 for 40 minutes until bubbling and golden.

PER SERVING 551 kcals, protein 21g, carbs 60g, fat 27g, sat fat 13g, fibre 4g, sugar 14g, salt 1.96g

Thai prawn, potato & vegetable curry

When freezing dishes with prawns in just check the packet first to make sure the ones you buy are suitable for home freezing.

❄️ • **TAKES 45 MINUTES** • **SERVES 8**

1 tbsp olive oil
4 tbsp Thai green curry paste
1 lemongrass stalk, outer layer removed, finely chopped
2 red peppers, deseeded and cut into chunky strips
450g/1lb baby new potatoes, halved
2 × 400g cans coconut milk
300ml/½ pint chicken stock
5 kaffir lime leaves, torn
1 bunch spring onions, sliced
225g/8oz frozen peas
600g/1lb 5oz raw king prawns
100g bag baby leaf spinach
2 tbsp Thai fish sauce
bunch coriander, leaves picked
juice 1 lime, plus extra wedges to serve (optional)

1 Heat the oil in a large frying pan or wok. Fry the curry paste and lemongrass for 1 minute, until fragrant. Tip in the peppers and new potatoes, then stir them to coat in the paste. Cook for 1–2 minutes. Pour in the coconut milk, stock and kaffir lime leaves, then bring to the boil. Simmer and cook for 15 minutes, until the potatoes are just tender.
2 Add the remaining ingredients, but if you're freezing don't add the spinach or coriander yet, and cook until the prawns turn pink, about 4 minutes. Serve, with some extra lime wedges, if you like, or cool before freezing in containers for up to 1 month. Defrost completely in the fridge before reheating and adding the spinach and coriander.

PER SERVING 324 kcals, protein 20g, carbs 18g, fat 20g, sat fat 15g, fibre 3g, sugar 7g, salt 1.97g

Fragrant fish tagine

To freeze, don't cook the fish in the sauce but freeze it separately then cook it when the sauce has been defrosted. Make half to eat now and half to freeze for another day.

❄ ● **TAKES 1 HOUR** ● **SERVES 8**

FOR THE CHERMOULA AND FISH

2 tbsp olive oil

4 garlic cloves, roughly chopped

4 tsp ground cumin

2 tsp paprika

bunch coriander, chopped

1 tsp salt

juice and zest 1 lemon

8 × 100g/4oz skinless tilapia fillets

FOR THE TAGINE

2 tbsp olive oil

2 large onions, halved and thinly sliced

2 garlic cloves, sliced

2 tsp each ground cumin and paprika

3 × 400g cans chopped tomatoes

500ml/18fl oz fish stock

175g/6oz pimiento-stuffed olives

4 green peppers, quartered, deseeded and sliced

500g bag baby new potatoes, halved lengthways

1 To make the chermoula, put the oil, garlic, cumin, paprika, three-quarters of the coriander and the salt in a small bowl. Add the lemon juice, then blitz with a hand blender until smooth. Spoon half over the fish fillets and turn them over to coat both sides. Set aside to marinate.

2 Heat the oil and fry the onions and garlic until softened and starting to colour, about 4–5 minutes. Add the cumin and paprika, and cook for 2 minutes more. Add the tomatoes, stock, olives and lemon zest, stir in the remaining chermoula and simmer, uncovered, for 10 minutes.

3 Stir in the peppers and potatoes, cover and simmer for 15 minutes until the potatoes are tender. If freezing, reserve half the sauce and chill before freezing.

4 Stir the remaining coriander into the tagine, then arrange the fish fillets on top (if freezing half, reserve four portions of fish), and cook for 4–6 minutes until the fish is just cooked.

PER SERVING 282 kcals, protein 24g, carbs 24g, fat 11g, sat fat 2g, fibre 5g, sugar 7g, salt 2.76g

Cottage chilli hotpot

This dish can defrost as you drive, so it makes a great first-night supper for a weekend away in a country cottage with friends.

❄ ● **TAKES 3 HOURS** ● **SERVES 6**

800g/1lb 12oz braising steak, cubed
2 tbsp plain flour, seasoned well
4 tbsp olive oil
300ml/½ pint red wine
2 red onions, roughly chopped
2 carrots, roughly chopped
4 garlic cloves, roughly chopped
2 red peppers, deseeded and cut into
  chunks
1 fresh red chilli, deseeded and sliced
few thyme sprigs, plus 1 tbsp leaves
1 bay leaf
1 tsp each ground cumin and coriander
½ tsp each ground cinnamon and chilli
  flakes
2 tsp caster or granulated sugar
2 × 400g cans chopped plum tomatoes
250ml/9fl oz good beef stock
400g can red kidney beans, drained
  and rinsed
1kg/2lb 4oz potatoes
knob of butter

1 Toss the beef in the flour, then brown half in a pan, using 1 tablespoon of the oil. Tip into a bowl. Add 100ml/3½fl oz of the wine to the pan and scrape up any bits on the bottom. Pour into the bowl with the cooked beef. Repeat.
2 Add 2 tablespoons of the oil to the pan and fry the veg, fresh chilli, thyme sprigs and bay for 10 minutes. Tip in the spices, cook for 1 minute, then add the rest of the wine and reduce by half. Add the sugar, tomatoes, beef and stock, then simmer for 1½–2 hours. Stir in the beans. Cool.
3 Peel and slice the potatoes, then boil for 5 minutes. Drain, then tip back into the pan. Stir in the butter and thyme leaves. Tip the chilli into a baking dish, then layer the potatoes on top. Dot with butter. Cover with cling film and cool completely if freezing. Will freeze for 1 month.
4 Heat oven to 200C/180C fan/gas 6 and bake for 50 minutes–1 hour, until the the potatoes are golden.

PER SERVING 584 kcals, protein 38g, carbs 55g, fat 23g, sat fat 8g, fibre 8g, sugar 16g, salt 1.27g

Saucy meatball & carrot bake with crispy feta crumbs

This recipe is perfectly suited to make some to eat now and freeze some for later.
It can be frozen for up to 3 months, but defrost completely before cooking.

❄ • **TAKES 1½ HOURS** • **SERVES 8**

900g/2lb minced pork
140g/5oz breadcrumbs
1 egg
1 tbsp caraway seeds
4 tsp ground cumin
750g/1lb 10oz carrots, peeled and
    halved lengthways, or quartered if
    they're really big
4 tbsp olive oil, plus extra for frying
3 onions, whizzed to a paste in a food
    processor
good chunk ginger, grated
680g bottle passata
2 × 400g cans chopped tomatoes
2 tbsp sugar
200g pack feta, crumbled
small pack parsley, chopped

1 Heat oven to 220C/200C fan/gas 7. Mix the pork, 50g/2oz of the breadcrumbs, egg, caraway seeds and half the cumin with 2 teaspoons salt and lots of pepper. Roll into 30 meatballs and put into a non-stick roasting tin. Put the carrots into another roasting tin. Split the oil between the two, and toss to coat. Roast for 30–40 minutes, shaking halfway through.
2 Meanwhile, fry the onions, ginger and remaining cumin in a drop more oil in a large pan, stirring constantly. Stir in the passata, tomatoes, sugar and some seasoning, then simmer for 15 minutes.
3 Divide the meatballs and carrots between the tins and spoon over the tomato sauce. Set aside any portions for freezing now and freeze.
4 To cook, heat oven to 200C/180C fan/gas 6. Mix the remaining breadcrumbs with the feta, parsley and some seasoning and sprinkle over. Bake for 20 minutes until piping hot.

PER SERVING 488 kcals, protein 33g, carbs 38g, fat 24g, sat fat 8g, fibre 5g, sugar 19g, salt 1.85g

Beef cannelloni

Batch-cooking at its best – portion this up to freeze in sizes that suit your household.
They'll keep in the freezer for up to 3 months, or you can chill them for up to 2 days.

❄ • **TAKES 2 HOURS** • **SERVES 12**

1kg/2lb 4oz lean minced beef
1 tbsp olive oil
1 large onion, finely chopped
4 garlic cloves, crushed
2 × 660g jars passata with basil
large pinch caster sugar
400g/14oz dried cannelloni tubes

FOR THE WHITE SAUCE

50g/2oz butter
50g/2oz plain flour
600ml/1 pint whole milk
140g/5oz soft cheese with garlic and
    herbs
140g/5oz Parmesan, grated

1 Dry-fry the beef in a non-stick pan on a medium–high heat until browned. Set aside. Add the oil and cook the onion for 5 minutes. Add the garlic for 1 minute more, then tip in the beef, 1½ jars of the passata sauce and the sugar. Simmer for 20 minutes.

2 Meanwhile, heat the butter for the sauce in a small pan. Stir in the flour. Add the milk gradually, stirring, then bubble for 2 minutes, still stirring. Remove from the heat and melt in the soft cheese. Season. Set aside, covered with cling film.

3 To assemble, pour the remaining passata into the base of two or three baking dishes or 12 individual ovenproof dishes. Spoon the beef into the cannelloni tubes and lay on top of the passata. Pour over the white sauce, then sprinkle with Parmesan. Allow to cool, then freeze.

4 Defrost and heat oven to 200C/180C fan/gas 6 and cook for 40 minutes until the pasta is tender.

PER SERVING 479 kcals, protein 31g, carbs 39g, fat 23g, sat fat 12g, fibre 2g, sugar 9g, salt 1.28g

Pork and chickpea curry

This hearty curry tastes even better if made a day before as the spices in the garlicky sauce will mellow and mature.

❄ ● **TAKES 2½ HOURS** ● **SERVES 8–10**

1½ tsp black peppercorns

2 tsp fennel seeds

1 tsp coriander seeds

2 tsp cumin seeds

1 tsp chilli powder

½ tsp turmeric

2 garlic bulbs, peeled, cloves separated

100ml/3½fl oz red wine vinegar

50ml/2 fl oz vegetable oil

3 large red onions, very finely chopped

1.5kg/3lb 5oz pork shoulder, cut into 1in pieces

2 red peppers, deseeded and roughly chopped

400g can chopped tomatoes

2 tsp dark muscovado sugar

2 × 400g cans chickpeas, drained and rinsed

450ml/16fl oz chicken stock

1 Tip the whole spices into a small food processor and add the chilli powder and turmeric. Add the garlic to the spices and process to a coarse paste. Drizzle in the vinegar while the motor is running. You can also use a mortar and pestle. Mix the spice paste with the pork and leave on one side for 15 minutes.

2 Heat oven to 150C/130C fan/gas 2.Heat the oil in a large pan and fry the onions until beginning to colour. Add the pork, turn the heat up high, and fry until darkened. Add the peppers, tomatoes and sugar and continue cooking for another 10 minutes until the tomatoes have cooked down. Stir in the chickpeas and stock. Cover, simmer, and transfer to the oven for about 1½ hours – until the meat is tender and the sauce thickened.

3 Serve with freshly boiled rice, or cool and freeze, in whichever sized batches suits you best. The curry will freeze for up to 5 months. Defrost completely before reheating.

PER SERVING 491 kcals, protein 33g, carbs 19g, fat 31g, sat fat 9g, fibre 4g, sugar 8g, salt 0.80g

Beef bourguignon

The secret to a great beef bourguignon is to use all wine and no stock. This wonderfully rich dish will keep in the freezer for up to 3 months.

❄ ● **TAKES 4 HOURS** ● **SERVES 6**

1.6kg/3lb 8oz braising steak, cut into large chunks
2 tbsp oil
3 large or 6 carrots, cut into large chunks
2 onions, roughly chopped
3 tbsp plain flour
1 tbsp tomato purée

FOR THE MARINADE

3 bay leaves
small bunch thyme
2 bottles cheap red wine

TO FINISH

small knob butter
300g/10oz bacon lardons
500g/1lb 2oz pearl onions or small shallots, peeled
400g/14oz mushrooms, halved
chopped parsley, to garnish

1 Cover the beef with the marinade ingredients; cover and chill overnight.
2 Heat oven to 200C/180C fan/gas 6. Put a colander over a large bowl and strain the marinated meat, keeping the liquid. Heat half the oil in a large frying pan, then brown the meat in batches. When all the meat is browned, pour a little reserved liquid into the frying pan and bubble briefly. Add to the meat.
3 Heat the rest of the oil in a casserole and fry the carrots and onions. Stir in the flour and tomato purée. Add the beef and the marinade liquid. Bring to a simmer then transfer to the oven and bake, covered, for 2 hours. Cool and freeze.
4 To serve, defrost completely and warm through. Meanwhile, heat the butter in a frying pan and fry the bacon and onions for 10 minutes. Add the mushrooms and fry for 5 minutes, then stir everything into the stew and heat for 10 minutes more. Serve scattered with chopped parsley.

PER SERVING 767 kcals, protein 67g, carbs 16g, fat 39g, sat fat 16g, fibre 4g, sugar 11g, salt 2.09g

Smoky aubergine dip

When serving lots of dishes it's always good to have a few dips that can be nibbled on to start or can be eaten with everything else.

TAKES 40 MINUTES • SERVES 8

2 aubergines
100g/4oz natural yogurt
juice ½ lemon
1 garlic clove
1 green chilli, chopped
1 tsp ground coriander
olive oil for drizzling
poppadums, to serve (optional)

1 Cook the aubergines whole on a barbecue or very hot griddle pan until the skin is blackened and the flesh soft, then leave to cool in a bowl. Peel off the charred skin and chop the flesh.

2 Tip into a food processor with the yogurt, lemon juice, garlic, chilli, coriander and olive oil, and season with salt and pepper. Blend until smooth, then tip into a bowl and drizzle with more olive oil. For a chunkier dip, the aubergine, garlic and chilli can be chopped by hand and mixed with the other ingredients.

3 The dip can be made a day ahead and chilled but is best served at room temperature. Serve with poppadoms, if you like.

PER SERVING 65 kcals, protein 2g, carbs 4g, fat 5g, sat fat 1g, fibre 2g, sugar 3g, salt 0.04g

Italian bean & olive salad

A lovely summery salad, perfect for outdoor entertaining or to serve as a side dish at a barbecue.

TAKES 30 MINUTES ● SERVES 8

2 yellow peppers
2 red peppers
300g/10oz green beans
300g/10oz cherry tomatoes, halved
1 tbsp small capers
2 handfuls black olives, stoned
4 tbsp olive oil
1 tbsp red wine vinegar
large bunch basil, leaves picked, large
    ones roughly shredded, small ones
    left whole

1 On the barbecue, under the grill or over a flame, blacken the peppers all over, then pop into a bowl and cover with cling film. Once cool, peel, deseed and cut into strips, keeping any juices.

2 Cook the beans in boiling salted water until crunchy but not squeaky, then drain and drop straight into iced water. Toss the beans with the peppers and all the remaining ingredients except the basil. The salad will sit at room temperature for a couple of hours or in the fridge overnight – just remove from the fridge several hours before serving to bring it up to room temperature.

3 To serve, gently stir through the shredded basil at the last minute, and scatter with the small basil leaves to finish.

PER SERVING 102 kcals, protein 2g, carbs 7g, fat 8g, sat fat 1g, fibre 3g, sugar 6g, salt 0.27g

Bacon-wrapped chicken drumsticks

This will be a crowd-pleaser at a buffet and is also easily transportable to take along on a picnic.

TAKES 1 HOUR • MAKES 12

juice 1 lemon, plus extra wedges to squeeze (optional)
2 garlic cloves, crushed
12 chicken drumsticks
12 rashers smoked streaky bacon
crusty baguette, to serve

1 Heat oven to 200C/180C fan/gas 6. Mix together the lemon juice and garlic with some seasoning. Prick the chicken several times with a sharp knife and drizzle with half the garlicky lemon juice. Wrap each drumstick in a rasher of bacon and put in a single layer in a roasting tin. Drizzle on the remaining garlicky lemon juice.
2 Roast for 45–50 minutes until the chicken is cooked through and the bacon is starting to crisp up. Flash under a hot grill if you like your bacon crisp.
3 Allow to cool, then chill until you're ready to serve – the drumsticks will keep in the fridge for 2 days. Eat with crusty bread and some extra lemon squeezed over the chicken, if you like.

PER SERVING (2 drumsticks) 286 kcals, protein 34g, carbs none, fat 17g, sat fat 6g, fibre none, sugar none, salt 1.45g

Mini sausage rolls

The secret to light sausage rolls is to add water to the sausage mix, which steams the pastry as it cooks. To cook from frozen, simply add 10 minutes to the cooking time.

❄ **UNCOOKED** ● **TAKES 1 HOUR**
● **MAKES 20**

½ small garlic clove
handful parsley, chopped
400g pack sausagemeat or sausages
   with skins removed
375g pack ready-rolled puff pastry
1 beaten egg, to glaze

1 Heat oven to 200C/180C fan/gas 6. Crush the garlic and a little salt to a paste using a pestle and mortar. Mix together with the parsley and stir in 50ml/2fl oz cold water. Put the sausagemeat in a food processor, turn on to a high speed, pour the garlic-flavoured water into the mixture, then season with pepper.
2 Cut the pastry in half lengthways. Divide the sausage mixture in two and spread along the length of each pastry strip in a cylinder shape, leaving a 1cm/½in edge. Tightly roll the pastry around the sausagemeat and brush the ends with the beaten egg. Use a sharp knife to cut each roll into 10 pieces, each about 2.5cm/1in long, and put on a baking sheet. Freeze for up to 1 month.
3 Brush more egg all over the pastry. Put in the oven and cook for 25–35 minutes until the pastry is puffed and crisp and the meat has cooked through. Remove and eat hot or cold.

PER ROLL 136 kcals, protein 4g, carbs 9g, fat 10g, sat fat 4g, fibre none, sugar 1g, salt 0.52g

Roasted tomato, basil & Parmesan quiche

A taste of summer, this quiche makes a great vegetarian option alongside salads and fresh bread. Get ahead and make it the night before it's needed.

TAKES 1 HOUR 20 MINUTES • CUTS INTO 8 SLICES

500g pack shortcrust pastry
plain flour, for dusting
300g/10oz cherry tomatoes
olive oil, for drizzling
2 eggs
300ml pot double cream
handful basil leaves, shredded, plus a few small ones left whole for scattering
50g/2oz Parmesan, grated

1 Roll out the pastry on a lightly floured surface to a round about 5cm/2in larger than a 25cm tin. Line the tart tin with the pastry, leaving an overhang of pastry. Chill for 20 minutes.

2 Heat oven to 200C/180C fan/gas 6. In a small roasting tin, drizzle the tomatoes with olive oil and season with salt and pepper. Put on a low shelf of the oven.

3 Prick the base of the tart then blind-bake for 20 minutes, remove the paper and beans, then continue to cook for 5–10 minutes until brown. Remove the tomatoes from the oven.

4 While the pastry is cooking, beat the eggs and gradually add the cream. Stir in the shredded basil and season. When the case is ready, sprinkle half the cheese over the base, scatter over the tomatoes, pour over the cream mix, then scatter over the rest of the cheese. Bake for 20–25 minutes. Cool in the tin and trim the pastry. Scatter over the reserved basil.

PER SLICE 494 kcals, protein 9g, carbs 29g, fat 39g, sat fat 22g, fibre 2g, sugar 2g, salt 0.48g

Sticky treacle-glazed ham

This ham is steam-roasted rather than boiled so you don't need gallons of water and an enormous pan – which most people don't own anyway!

❄ **LEFTOVERS** ● **TAKES 3½ HOURS**
● **SERVES 8**

3.5–4kg/7lb 10oz–9lb boned and rolled piece unsmoked ham
2 oranges, 1 cut into wedges, zest and juice 1
1 cinnamon stick
2 tbsp English mustard
85g/3oz black treacle
handful cloves

1 Heat oven to 180C/160C fan/gas 4. Put the ham, skin-side up, in a roasting tin, then add enough water to cover the base. Scatter the orange wedges and cinnamon stick around. Tightly cover the pan with foil, then cook for 2½ hours.

2 Meanwhile, mix the mustard, treacle and orange zest together with enough orange juice to make a mixture loose enough to paint over the ham.

3 When the ham has cooked, remove the roasting tin from the oven and turn up the heat to 220C/200C fan/gas 7. Remove the foil, leave the ham until cool enough to handle, then pour away any liquid. Carefully cut away the skin to leave an even layer of fat. Score the ham in a diamond pattern, paint the glaze over the fat, then stud with cloves.

4 Roast the ham for 30 minutes until glazed. Leave to cool, then either leave at room temperature overnight or keep in the fridge for 3 days.

PER SERVING 707 kcals, protein 78g, carbs 6g, fat 42g, sat fat 16g, fibre none, sugar 6g, salt 9.97g

Red rice & chicken with pomegranate & feta

Shop-bought roast chickens are perfect for shredding into salads. This makes enough for a big bowl and keeps overnight in the fridge.

TAKES 45 MINUTES • SERVES 6, AS PART OF A BUFFET

250g/9oz red Camargue rice
zest and juice 2 lemons
4 tbsp extra virgin olive oil
pinch caster sugar
1 small ready-roasted chicken, skin discarded and meat shredded
50g/2oz almonds, toasted and chopped
1 medium cucumber, deseeded, cut into diagonal chunky pieces
1 bunch spring onions, chopped
100g/4oz feta, crumbled
1 pomegranate, seeds removed
small handful dill, finely chopped

1 Boil the rice in plenty of salted water until just cooked, about 30 minutes.
2 Meanwhile, make the dressing and prepare the other ingredients. Put the lemon zest and juice and olive oil in a jam jar with a fitted lid. Add some seasoning and the sugar, and shake well.
3 Drain the cooled rice and tip into a large bowl. Pour the dressing over the warm rice and mix well. Let it soak in a little, then toss through the rest of the ingredients, except the dill. The salad can now be covered and kept in the fridge for up to 1 day. To serve, simply add the dill and give everything a mix.

PER SERVING 922 kcals, protein 69g, carbs 56g, fat 48g, sat fat 13g, fibre 3g, sugar 8g, salt 4.07g

Squash & barley salad with balsamic vinaigrette

Barley makes a fantastically textured salad and has the added bonus of being one of the healthiest grains there is.

TAKES 30 MINUTES • SERVES 8

1 butternut squash, peeled and cut into long pieces
1 tbsp olive oil
250g/9oz pearl barley
300g/10oz thin-stem broccoli, cut into medium-size pieces
100g/4oz SunBlush tomatoes, sliced
1 small red onion, diced
2 tbsp pumpkin seeds
1 tbsp small capers, rinsed
15 black olives, pitted
20g pack basil, chopped

FOR THE DRESSING

5 tbsp balsamic vinegar
6 tbsp extra virgin olive oil
1 tbsp Dijon mustard
1 garlic clove, finely chopped

1 Heat oven to 200C/180C fan/gas 6. Put the squash on a baking sheet and toss with olive oil. Roast for 20 minutes. Meanwhile, boil the barley for about 25 minutes in salted water until tender but al dente.

2 Meanwhile, whisk the dressing ingredients in a small bowl, then season with salt and pepper. Drain the barley, then tip it into a bowl and pour over the dressing. Mix well and let it cool.

3 Boil the broccoli in salted water until just tender, then drain and rinse in cold water. Drain and pat dry. Add the broccoli and remaining ingredients to the barley and mix well. This will keep for 2 days in the fridge and is delicious warm or cold.

PER SERVING 301 kcals, protein 6g, carbs 40g, fat 14g, sat fat 2g, fibre 4g, sugar 9g, salt 0.55g

Lemon & honey chicken

Cook the chicken at least the day before, but leave the slicing until you are ready to serve in order to keep it moist.

❄ • **TAKES 1 HOUR** • **SERVES 6–8**

6–8 boneless skinless chicken breasts (about 1kg/2lb 4oz in total)

2 tbsp clear honey

grated zest 2 lemons, juice 1

2 tbsp olive oil

1 curly lettuce, such as Batavia or Webb's

1 Heat oven to 190C/170C fan/gas 5. Arrange the chicken in a shallow ovenproof dish. Mix together the honey, lemon zest and juice, oil, salt and pepper, then pour over the chicken breasts and turn them around until well coated.

2 Roast the chicken breasts for 40–45 minutes, turning them halfway through the cooking time and basting, occasionally, until they are golden brown and shiny and the marinade has almost evaporated. Leave to cool, then wrap in foil and chill until ready to eat. The chicken may now be frozen for up to 1 month.

3 If freezing, remove from the freezer and allow to defrost thoroughly. Before serving, spread the lettuce over a large platter, tearing up any large leaves. Slice the chicken breasts, keeping them together, then arrange over the lettuce.

PER SERVING (6) 229 kcals, protein 40g, carbs 5g, fat 6g, sat fat 1g, fibre none, added sugar 4g, salt 0.26g

Foil-poached salmon

The onion is in the centre of the salmon purely to flavour the flesh, so don't be tempted to serve it as it will barely be cooked.

TAKES 1 HOUR 20 MINUTES
● **SERVES 10**

3.5kg/7lb 10oz whole salmon (ask your fishmonger to clean and gut it)
olive oil, for greasing
1 small onion, very thinly sliced
4 bay leaves
handful dill sprigs
6 tbsp dry white wine

TO GARNISH
bunch watercress, lemon wedges, thick cucumber slices, fresh dill (optional)

1 Heat oven to 150C/130C fan/gas 2. Put the salmon on a large sheet of oiled extra-wide foil (the oil will stop it from sticking later). Put the onion, bay leaves and dill in the body cavity, spoon over the wine, season with salt and black pepper, then loosely bring the foil round the salmon and seal well to make a parcel. Lift on to a baking sheet and bake for 1 hour. Leave to cool in its parcel. This can be done a day ahead and chilled.
2 Unwrap the salmon, then strip away the skin and fins from the top. You can leave the head on or take it off at this stage. Carefully lift the fish on to a platter, then garnish with watercress, cucumber, lemon wedges and dill, if using.
3 To serve, remove the fish in chunky fillets. When all the fish has gone from the top fillet, remove the onion and herb flavouring, pull away the bones, then remove portions of the bottom fillet, leaving the skin behind.

PER SERVING 612 kcals, protein 45g, carbs 2g, fat 47g, sat fat 8g, fibre 2g, sugar 1g, salt 0.49g

Double cheese & onion soufflé tart

This recipe is really useful. Serve as a starter or main course, as part of a summer buffet or pack it up for a picnic. It can be made a day ahead.

TAKES 1 HOUR 25 MINUTES

● **SERVES 8**

375g pack shortcrust pastry
75g/2½oz Parmesan, grated
4 tbsp onion chutney
50g/2oz butter
50g/2oz plain flour
300ml/½ pint milk
300g/10oz soft rindless goat's cheese
1 tbsp thyme, leaves only, chopped
3 eggs, separated

1 Heat oven to 200C/180C fan/gas 6. Roll the pastry out until almost large enough to line a 22cm loose-bottomed tart tin, sprinkle over a third of the Parmesan, continue rolling to push the cheese in. Line the tin, leaving an overhang. Bake blind for 20 minutes. Remove the baking beans and bake for a further 10 minutes.

2 Spread the chutney over the bottom of the pastry case. Melt the butter in a pan over a low heat, add the flour and cook for 2 minutes. Slowly pour in the milk, stirring until thickened. Take off the heat.

3 Crumble 200g/7oz of goat's cheese, the thyme and the rest of the Parmesan into the sauce. Beat until the cheese melts, then beat in the egg yolks one by one. Whisk the egg whites to peaks, stir 1 spoonful into the sauce and mix, then gently fold in the rest.

4 Spoon the filling on to the chutney, crumble over the remaining goat's cheese and bake for 25–30 minutes. Cool slightly before trimming the edges.

PER SERVING 456 kcals, protein 16g, carbs 32g, fat 30g, sat fat 15g, fibre 1g, sugar 5g, salt 1.38g

New potato & frisée salad

Homemade salad cream is so much more delicious than shop-bought and will keep for up to a week in the fridge.

TAKES 45 MINUTES ● SERVES 10

1.5kg/3lb 5oz baby new potatoes, larger ones halved

bunch chives, snipped

1 frisée lettuce, torn into bite-size pieces

FOR THE SALAD CREAM

1 tbsp plain flour

4 tsp caster sugar

2 tsp mustard powder

2 eggs

100ml/3½fl oz white wine vinegar

150ml/¼ pint double cream

squeeze lemon juice

1 Boil the potatoes in salted water until tender, about 15 minutes. Drain well in a colander and steam-dry for 5–10 minutes.

2 Make the salad cream by mixing the flour, sugar, mustard powder and some seasoning in a bowl, then beat in the eggs and white wine vinegar. Put the bowl over a pan of simmering water, making sure the base does not touch the water, and stir continuously until it thickens enough to coat the back of a spoon, about 5–10 minutes.

3 Remove from the heat and cool. Add the cream and lemon juice to taste. Cover and chill until you are ready to dress the potatoes. Everything can be prepared up to 2 days in advance at this stage.

4 Toss the potatoes in the salad cream along with most of the chives. Arrange the frisée on a platter or in a large bowl. Spoon over the potatoes and scatter with the rest of the chives.

PER SERVING 266 kcals, protein 6g, carbs 34g, fat 13g, sat fat 6g, fibre 2g, sugar 5g, salt 0.13g

Fidget pie

Fidget pie – or fidgety pie – is like a big pork pie that can take centre stage on a traditional British buffet table. It keeps well if made the day before.

TAKES 1½ HOURS ● SERVES 8

FOR THE PASTRY

500g/1lb 2oz plain flour, plus extra for dusting
140g/5oz lard
butter, for the tin
1 egg, beaten for glazing

FOR THE FILLING

500g/1lb 2oz minced pork
125ml/4fl oz medium English cider
4 sage leaves, finely chopped
¼ tsp ground mace
1 tbsp brown sugar
100g/4oz unsmoked bacon, finely chopped
225g/8oz grated onion
225g/8oz peeled grated apple (half cooker, half eater is best)
1 large potato, grated

1 Tip the flour into a large bowl with 1 teaspoon salt. Heat the lard and 210ml/7fl oz water until the lard melts and the water is simmering. Pour into the flour and bring together. Tip onto a floured surface and knead. Cover and set aside.

2 Mix the pork, cider, 1 teaspoon salt, sage, mace and sugar for the filling in a bowl. Add the bacon, onion, apple and potato. Mix well with your hands.

3 Heat oven to 200C/180C fan/gas 6. Put a 22cm springform cake tin, minus its base, on a baking sheet. Line the bottom of the tin with greaseproof paper and butter the sides. Roll out two-thirds of the pastry to a large circle and line the tin, allowing some overlap. Roll the reserved pastry to form a lid.

4 Put the filling in the case and push it down hard. Brush the pastry edges with water and cover with the lid. Crimp together and brush with egg. Bake for 1 hour, turn off the heat and leave in the oven for 30 minutes. Cool before eating.

PER SERVING 578 kcals, protein 22g, carbs 61g, fat 29g, sat fat 12g, fibre 3g, sugar 8g, salt 1.80g

Asparagus, sun-dried tomato & olive loaf

Make sure vegetarians don't feel left out of the party with this stunning centrepiece.

TAKES 1 HOUR • CUTS INTO 10 SLICES

100ml/3½fl oz olive oil, plus extra for greasing
250g/9oz asparagus spears, each cut into 3 pieces
200g/7oz self-raising flour
1 tbsp thyme leaves
3 large eggs, lightly beaten
100ml/3½fl oz milk
handful pitted black olives
100g/4oz sun-dried tomatoes, roughly chopped
100g/4oz Gruyère or Beaufort, grated

1 Heat oven to 190C/170C fan/gas 5. Oil and line the base of a loaf tin (about 22 × 10 × 5cm) with baking paper. Cook the asparagus in boiling salted water for 2 minutes, drain, then cool quickly under cold running water. Pat dry.

2 Mix the flour and thyme with some seasoning in a large bowl. Make a well in the centre, then add the eggs, milk and oil, stirring all the time to draw the flour into the centre. Beat for 1 minute to make a smooth batter.

3 Reserve five asparagus tips and a few olives. Add the remaining asparagus and olives, the tomatoes and two-thirds of the cheese to the batter. Pour into the tin, then put the reserved asparagus and olives on top. Sprinkle with the remaining cheese. Bake for 35–40 minutes until the loaf feels firm to the touch and is golden and crusty on top. Cool in the tin for 5 minutes, then turn out and cool on a wire rack. The loaf can be made the day before. Serve cut into slices.

PER SLICE 317 kcals, protein 11g, carbs 22g, fat 21g, sat fat 5g, fibre 3g, sugar 3g, salt 1.04g

Roasted sirloin of beef with salsa verde

A buffet-friendly take on the Sunday roast beef, with the added twist of a zingy salsa verde on the side.

TAKES 1 HOUR ● SERVES 8–10

1.5kg/3lb 5oz sirloin of beef
1 tbsp olive oil
rocket leaves, to garnish

FOR THE SALSA VERDE

2 tbsp capers, drained, rinsed and
    chopped
2 tbsp gherkins, finely chopped
½ bunch spring onions, finely chopped
small bunch parsley, finely chopped
juice 2 lemons
4 tbsp extra virgin olive oil

1 Heat oven to 240C/220C fan/gas 9. Rub the beef all over with the oil and season with some salt and lots of black pepper. Transfer to a roasting tin and cook for 20 minutes, then turn the oven to 190C/170C fan/gas 5 and roast for a further 10–15 minutes per 450g/1lb for medium–rare, 15–20 minutes for medium, 20–25 minutes for medium–well and 25–30 minutes for well done. Remove from the oven and allow to cool. The beef can be roasted up to 2 days before.
2 To make the salsa verde, mix all the ingredients with some salt and pepper – this can be done up to 2 days in advance and chilled.
3 To serve, thinly slice the beef and arrange on a serving platter, drizzle with the salsa verde and scatter over the rocket leaves.

PER SERVING (8) 353 kcals, protein 38g, carbs 1g, fat 22g, sat fat 8g, fibre none, sugar none, salt 0.41g

Garland sausage roll slice

Remind everyone just how good this retro free-form pie can actually be when it's home-made with quality ingredients. Make it a day ahead and keep chilled.

TAKES 1¼ HOURS • CUTS INTO 8–10

18 quail's eggs
650g/1lb 7oz Cumberland sausages, split and squeezed
1 small onion, grated
1 Bramley apple, peeled and grated
small bunch flat-leaf parsley, leaves chopped
shake of Tabasco sauce
1cm/½in-thick slice of ham, cut into small chunks
50g/2oz fresh breadcrumbs
500g pack all-butter puff pastry
1 egg, beaten
wholegrain mustard, to serve

1 Cook the eggs in a pan of boiling water for 2½ minutes, then cool slightly before peeling and trimming each end.

2 Heat oven to 220C/200C fan/gas 7. In a bowl, mix together the sausagemeat, grated onion, apple, parsley, Tabasco, ham and breadcrumbs. Roll the pastry to a rectangle about 25 × 35cm, lift on to a baking sheet and brush with beaten egg.

3 Press two-thirds of the sausage mix along one of the long sides of the pastry, leaving 2cm/¾in pastry free on one side, and half of the pastry empty on the other side for folding over later. Press a line down the middle of the meat with your finger, then lay the eggs along it. Press over the rest of the sausagemeat. Fold the pastry over the filling and press the edges together, then trim with a knife and seal well by pressing the edges.

4 Brush all over with more egg and bake for 40 minutes until golden. Leave to cool. Slice and serve with mustard.

PER SLICE (8) 564 kcals, protein 26g, carbs 33g, fat 37g, sat fat 16g, fibre 1g, sugar 4g, salt 2.66g

Gazpacho

This is gazpacho the way it should be – dazzling red and smooth enough to drink from a glass.

TAKES 30 MINUTES • SERVES 8

1 red onion, chopped
2 garlic cloves, finely chopped
1 red pepper, deseeded and chopped
4 ripe tomatoes, chopped
1 slice white bread, crusts removed
   and torn
500g/18oz passata
300ml/½ pint vegetable stock
5 tbsp olive oil, plus extra for drizzling
4 tbsp wine vinegar
1 tsp Tabasco sauce or harissa
1 tsp sugar
torn basil leaves, to garnish

1 Put the onion, garlic, pepper, tomatoes and bread in a food processor and blend until finely chopped, but not too smooth. Tip into a large bowl with the passata, stock, oil, vinegar, Tabasco or harissa, sugar and some seasoning. Mix well, cover the bowl with cling film or foil and put in the fridge for at least 2 hours or up to 2 days.

2 To serve, pour into eight small bowls or glasses, drizzle over a little olive oil and sprinkle with a few torn basil leaves.

PER SERVING 134 kcals, protein 2g, carbs 11g, fat 10g, sat fat 1g, fibre 1g, sugar 6g, salt 0.48g

Spiced crab on toast

Put a large jar of this lovely starter in the middle of the table and let everyone help themselves.

TAKES 30 MINUTES ● SERVES 6

300g/10oz prepared crab, fresh or frozen (defrosted)
175g/6oz butter
1 red chilli, deseeded and finely chopped
juice 1 lemon
½ tsp freshly grated nutmeg
1 bay leaf
18–20 large cooked prawns in their shells
bunch radishes
rustic bread, such as sourdough, toasted, to serve

1 Tip the crab into a bowl and check for any pieces of shell. Melt 100g/4oz of the butter and add half the chilli, the lemon juice, nutmeg and some salt. Add to the crab and mix well. Pack into a bowl or jar, pressing down lightly.

2 Melt the remaining butter. When it is foaming, remove from the heat. When the foam has died down, carefully skim off any scum that is on the surface with a teaspoon, then pour the clear butter over the crab, leaving behind any milky sediment. Scatter over the remaining chilli and put a bay leaf in the centre.

3 Leave to set in the fridge for at least 1 hour or until the following day. Serve on a board with the prawns and radishes, and slices of toasted bread.

PER SERVING 283 kcals, protein 10g, carbs 1g, fat 27g, sat fat 16g, fibre none, sugar none, salt 0.89g

Pork & pistachio terrine

Terrines look very cheffy but are actually simple to put together and make a great starter for a large table.

❄ • **TAKES 1½ HOURS** • **SERVES 10**

12–18 rashers smoked streaky bacon
3 large garlic cloves, sliced
25g/1oz butter
800g/1lb 12oz minced pork
50g/2oz pistachio nuts
1 tsp salt
3 tbsp fresh thyme leaves
25g/1oz dried cranberries
3 tbsp brandy
1 large egg, beaten
200/7oz fresh chicken livers

1 Heat oven to 180C/160C fan/gas 4. Line a 900g loaf tin with 6–12 rashers of the bacon, slightly overlapping them and letting the excess hang over the top.
2 Fry the garlic in the butter for just a minute, cool briefly, then mix with all the other ingredients except the livers. Season with plenty of black pepper.
3 Press half the mince mixture into the tin, then lay the livers on top. Cover with the remaining mince mixture, then top with the remaining 6 bacon rashers. Fold over the overhanging bacon.
4 Bake for 1¼ hours, then pour off most of the liquid. Cover with foil and put a weight on top of the terrine as it cools to compact the texture. As soon as it is cool enough, put in the fridge. It will keep there for 3 days. To freeze, cool completely, then wrap with cling film, then foil. Use within 6 weeks. Thaw for 24 hours in the fridge. To serve, turn out of the tin or unwrap and cut into slices.

PER SERVING 294 kcals, protein 25g, carbs 3g, fat 19g, sat fat 7g, fibre none, sugar 2g, salt 1.50g

Velvety duck liver parfait

Very impressive and completely make ahead – perfect to spread on toast with some chutney and gherkins. Freeze the finished dish for 1 month and defrost to serve.

❄️ • **TAKES 45 MINUTES** • **SERVES 6**

600g/1lb 5oz duck or chicken livers, or a mix of both
250g pack butter, diced and slightly softened
2 shallots, finely sliced
1 garlic clove, sliced
splash each brandy and port
1 tbsp tomato purée
toast, to serve

FOR THE TOPPING
100g/4oz butter
1 tbsp thyme leaves
1 tsp cracked black peppercorns

1 Cut away and discard any sinews from the livers. Heat about a third of the butter in a frying pan, then fry the shallots and garlic for 3–4 minutes. Turn up the heat, add the livers, then fry until just browned. Add the brandy and port, and boil down quickly. Remove from the heat and cool.

2 Season the livers, then tip everything into a food processor with the tomato purée and remaining butter, and blitz until smooth. Push the mixture through a sieve into a bowl then tip into a serving dish. Put in the fridge to set.

3 Once the mixture has set, gently melt the butter for the topping in a pan or in the microwave, then leave to settle and separate. Pour the yellow butter that has risen to the top into another bowl and discard the milky liquid. Leave the yellow butter to cool slightly, then mix in the thyme and peppercorns. Pour the mixture over the parfait and leave to set in the fridge. You can make the parfait up to 2 days ahead. Serve with warm toast.

PER SERVING 535 kcals, protein 18g, carbs 2g, fat 50g, sat fat 31g, fibre none, sugar 1g, salt 1.11g

Mushroom butter on toast

This make-ahead starter delivers all the flavour of mushrooms on toast without any last-minute frying.

❄ • **TAKES 35 MINUTES** • **SERVES 8**

250g pack butter, softened
1 onion, very finely chopped
3 garlic cloves, finely chopped
2 thyme sprigs, plus extra to garnish
30g pack dried porcini mushrooms,
    soaked, drained and finely chopped
250g pack chestnut mushrooms,
    finely chopped
2 tbsp brandy
juice ½ lemon
small handful each parsley and
    tarragon, finely chopped
toasted bread and salad leaves,
    to serve

1 Melt 50g/2oz of the butter in a pan and gently fry the onion until softened. Add the garlic and thyme, and fry for 1 minute more. Tip in all the mushrooms and toss to coat in the butter. Cook on a high heat for 5–8 minutes until soft. Pour over the brandy and lemon juice, then cook for 2–3 minutes more or until all the liquid has evaporated. Turn off the heat, add the herbs and some seasoning, then allow to cool.

2 Once cooled, remove the thyme. Mix the mushrooms with the remaining butter, then divide among four ramekins. Chill until firm, or for up to 2 days, or freeze for up to 3 months. Defrost completely before serving.

3 Serve a ramekin, topped with a thyme sprig, to share between two people, along with freshly toasted bread and dressed salad leaves.

PER SERVING 266 kcals, protein 2g, carbs 4g, fat 26g, sat fat 16g, fibre 2g, sugar 1g, salt 0.39g

Potted ham

This is a great way to use up leftover ham. If you don't have individual pots, the mix can be set in a loaf tin lined with cling film.

❄ • **TAKES 35 MINUTES** • **SERVES 8**

250g pack unsalted butter
500g/1lb 2oz cooked ham
bunch curly parsley, leaves picked
    and finely chopped
small pinch ground cloves
pinch yellow mustard seeds
1 tbsp cider vinegar
rustic country bread toast, cornichons,
    chutney or red onion marmalade,
    to serve

1 Gently melt the butter in a small pan and leave it to settle. Slowly pour the clear yellow fat from the melted butter into a small bowl or jug, leaving the milky liquid in the pan. Discard the milky bit. Pull apart and shred the ham as finely as possible into stringy strips – use a knife to help if you need to.

2 Mix the ham with the parsley, spices, vinegar, two-thirds of the butter and a little crunchy sea salt. Divide among eight small ramekins or pots. Press down and flatten the surface with your fingers, then spoon or pour over the remaining butter. Chill until the butter is solid, then wrap in cling film. Will freeze for up to 3 months.

3 To serve, defrost the pots overnight in the fridge if frozen. Serve in the pot or dip pots briefly in a bowl of hot water and turn the potted ham out on to plates. Serve with toast, cornichons and chutney or red onion marmalade.

PER SERVING 316 kcals, protein 14g, carbs 1g, fat 29g, sat fat 17g, fibre none, sugar 5g, salt 2.05g

Baked goat's cheese with hazelnut crust & balsamic onions

This makes a very easy starter and can be made ahead and frozen. As a change from the onions, you could serve the nutty cheese with a crisp apple salad.

❄ ● **TAKES 55 MINUTES** ● **SERVES 6**

3 × 100g goat's cheese (we used
    Capricorn)
50g/2oz hazelnuts, chopped
25g/1oz breadcrumbs
2 eggs, beaten
red chicory leaves, watercress and
    rocket, to serve

FOR THE ONIONS

3 tbsp olive oil
3 red onions, halved and thinly sliced
4 tbsp balsamic vinegar
4 tbsp mild-flavoured clear honey

1 Halve the goat's cheeses horizontally and mix the nuts with the breadcrumbs. Coat the cheese in the egg, then the nut mixture. Mark the cut-side of the cheese with a large piece of nut to show which side up it should be.

2 Heat the oil in a non-stick pan, then add the onions. Cook for 10 minutes until softened. Tip in the vinegar and honey, season and stir until syrupy. Freeze the cheeses until solid, then wrap individually. Pack the onions into a freezer bag once cool. To defrost, thaw the onions and warm gently in a pan.

3 To cook, heat oven to 200C/180C fan/ gas 6. Put the cheese on some baking parchment on a baking sheet and bake for 20 minutes. If you're cooking from frozen, add another 5 minutes. Arrange the salad leaves on plates and spoon the onions on top. Add the goat's cheese and serve immediately.

PER SERVING 366 kcals, protein 14g, carbs 17g, fat 28g, sat fat 11g, fibre 1g, sugar 12g, salt 1.05g

Salmon coulibiac

You can make this delicious and hearty dish a day in advance, leaving the coulibiac on the baking sheet and simply cooking it when it's needed.

TAKES 2½ HOURS ● SERVES 6

50g/2oz butter
700g/1lb 9oz boneless skinless lightly smoked salmon fillets, cut into thick slices
2 × 375g blocks puff pastry
4 hard-boiled eggs, sliced
1 egg, beaten, for glazing

FOR THE RICE

1 large onion, finely chopped
1 tsp cumin seeds
1 tsp coriander seeds
4 cardamom pods
2 star anise
200g/7oz basmati rice
1 bay leaf
4cm/1½in piece cinnamon stick
400ml/14fl oz fish stock or water
zest 1 lemon, juice ½
large bunch dill, chopped

1 Heat half the butter in a pan and cook the salmon for 2 minutes. Set aside. Melt the rest of the butter and fry the onion, cumin, coriander, cardamom and star anise for 8 minutes. Stir in the rice, bay leaf, cinnamon stick and stock. Cover, boil, then lower the heat for 10 minutes. Turn off the heat, stand for 10 minutes and add the zest and juice. Cool and add the dill.

2 Roll out one block of pastry to a rectangle as wide as a magazine but a third longer. Lay on a baking sheet. Pack half the rice along the middle, discarding the star anise and cinnamon, and leaving a 5cm border. Lay the salmon over the rice, then the eggs, then top with the reserved rice. Brush the border with beaten egg.

3 Roll out the remaining pastry to a slightly larger rectangle. Drape over the coulibiac and press the edges to seal.

4 Heat oven to 220C/200C fan/gas 7. Brush the pie with egg, score, then bake for 20 minutes. Reduce the heat slightly and cook for another 20 minutes.

PER SERVING 917 kcals, protein 47g, carbs 73g, fat 51g, sat fat 29g, fibre 3g, sugar 3g, salt 7.63g

Toulouse sausage cassoulet

This French bake is perfect for economical entertaining on winter evenings. Before cooking, it can be frozen for 2 months – just defrost prior to baking.

❄ ● **TAKES 1½ HOURS** ● **SERVES 4–6**

2 tbsp olive oil

2 onions, chopped

2 carrots, chopped

4 garlic cloves, crushed

4 tomatoes, chopped

bundle fresh parsley, thyme and bay leaf, tied together with string

2 × 400g cans haricot beans, rinsed and drained

300ml/½ pint white wine

12 Toulouse sausages

100g/4oz breadcrumbs, made from stale bread

1 Heat 1 tablespoon of the olive oil in a large pan, add the chopped onions, carrots, 3 garlic cloves, tomatoes, herb bundle and some salt and pepper. Cook over a gentle heat for 5 minutes, then stir in the beans, wine and 200m/7fl ozl water. Boil, then simmer for 5 minutes.

2 In a large frying pan, add the remaining olive oil and brown the sausages all over.

3 Rub the inside of a baking dish with the remaining garlic clove. Pour in half the bean mix, arrange the sausages on top, then finish with another layer of beans. The dish can now be chilled for up to 2 days or frozen.

4 To cook, heat oven to 180C/160C fan/ gas 4. Cover with foil and put in the oven for 45 minutes. Remove the dish from the oven, discard the foil and sprinkle the breadcrumbs over the top. Return to the oven and bake for a 20 minutes more until the breadcrumbs are golden and crusty.

PER SERVING (4) 623 kcals, protein 36g, carbs 31g, fat 39g, sat fat 14g, fibre 10g, sugar 11g, salt 2.33g

Wintry vegetable crumbles

These warming vegetarian crumbles can be made and frozen ahead for up to 3 months. An ideal make-ahead meal for a cosy dinner with friends.

❄ • **TAKES 1½ HOURS** • **MAKES 6**

FOR THE FILLING

400ml/14fl oz vegetable stock
450g/1lb celeriac, peeled and diced
3 carrots, peeled and diced
2 small sweet potatoes, peeled and diced
2 leeks, sliced
200ml tub crème fraîche
2 tbsp plain flour
1 tbsp wholegrain mustard
1 tsp thyme leaves

FOR THE CRUMBLE

50g/2oz butter, diced
50g/2oz plain flour
50g/2oz ground almonds
50g/2oz Parmesan, grated
25g/1oz flaked almonds

1 Pour the stock into a pan and bring to the boil. Tip in the celeriac, carrots and sweet potatoes, then add the leeks. Cover the pan and cook for 10 minutes.

2 Beat the crème fraîche with the flour and mustard. Stir into the vegetables until thickened, then add the thyme and season. Remove from the heat.

3 For the crumble, rub the butter into the flour and ground almonds. Season, then stir in the Parmesan and flaked almonds. Spoon the filling into six small ovenproof dishes and scatter the crumble on top. The crumbles can be assembled 1 day ahead and chilled. To freeze, wrap in cling film, then foil. To defrost, thaw overnight in the fridge.

4 To cook, heat oven to 190C/170C fan/ gas 5 and bake for 30–35 minutes until golden and slightly crisp.

PER CRUMBLE 433 kcals, protein 10g, carbs 30g, fat 31g, sat fat 15g, fibre 8g, sugar 11g, salt 0.81g

Minced beef Wellington

Love beef Wellington but can't stomach the price of fillet steak? Well, here's a budget-friendly makeover. It can be made a day in advance before cooking.

TAKES 1½ HOURS ● SERVES 8

1kg/2lb 4oz minced beef
100g/4oz tomato ketchup
4 eggs
3 onions, finely chopped
3 garlic cloves, finely chopped
small handful sage, chopped
handful parsley, chopped
25g/1oz butter
200g/7oz mushrooms, finely chopped
500g pack puff pastry

1 Thoroughly mix the beef with the ketchup, 3 eggs, some seasoning and 100ml/3½fl oz water. Mix in the onions, half the garlic and herbs.
2 Heat oven to 200C/180C fan/gas 6. Press the meat into a sausage shape about 30 × 10cm/12 × 4in on a baking sheet. Cook for 20 minutes then cool.
3 Heat the butter in a frying pan and cook the mushrooms for 3 minutes. Add the remaining garlic and cook for 2 minutes, pouring off any excess liquid.
4 Roll the pastry into a rectangle large enough to wrap up the beef. Beat the remaining egg with a little water and brush the pastry. Spread the mushroom mix into a strip along the middle of the pastry. Sit the meat on top then cut the pastry either side into strips. Criss-cross these over the meat.
5 Heat oven to 200C/180C fan/gas 6. Brush with more egg, then put on a baking sheet and cook for 40 minutes.

PER SERVING 640 kcals, protein 33g, carbs 27g, fat 45g, sat fat 20g, fibre 2g, sugar 7g, salt 1.42g

Irish stew

The trick with this classic slow-cook one-pot is to use a cheaper cut of meat, which means you'll skimp on price but not quality.

TAKES 2½ HOURS ● SERVES 6

1 tbsp sunflower oil
200g/7oz smoked streaky bacon, preferably in one piece, skinned and cut into chunks
900g/2lb stewing lamb, cut into large chunks
5 medium onions, sliced
5 carrots, sliced into chunks
3 bay leaves
small bunch thyme
100g/4oz pearl barley
850ml/1½ pints lamb stock
6 medium potatoes, cut into chunks
small knob of butter
3 spring onions, finely sliced

1 Heat oven to 160C/140C fan/gas 3. Heat the oil in a flameproof casserole. Sizzle the bacon for 4 minutes until crisp. Turn up the heat, then cook the lamb for 6 minutes until brown. Remove the meats with a slotted spoon. Add the onions, carrots and herbs to the pan, then cook for about 5 minutes until softened. Return the meat to the pan, stir in the pearl barley, pour over the stock, then bring to a simmer.
2 Sit the chunks of potato on top of the stew, cover, then braise in the oven, undisturbed, for about 1½ hours until the potatoes are soft and the meat is tender. The stew can now be chilled and kept in the fridge for 2 days, then reheated in a low oven or on top of the stove. Remove from the oven, dot the potatoes with butter, scatter with the spring onions and serve scooped straight from the dish.

PER SERVING 627 kcals, protein 49g, carbs 44g, fat 30g, sat fat 14g, fibre 5g, sugar 11g, salt 2.13g

Tender duck & pineapple red curry

This slow-cooked curry improves if made up to 2 days ahead, without the pineapple.
Simply add the pineapple and reheat.

TAKES 2½ HOURS ● SERVES 6

6 duck legs
2 tbsp light soft brown sugar
4 tbsp Thai red curry paste
400ml can coconut milk
2 tbsp fish sauce, plus extra to taste
6 kaffir lime leaves
1 small pineapple, peeled, cored and
    cut into chunks
1 red chilli, deseeded and finely sliced
    (optional)
bunch Thai basil leaves (optional)
plain boiled rice, to serve

1 Heat oven to 180C/160C fan/gas 4. Dry-fry the duck legs in an ovenproof frying pan or casserole dish on a low heat for 10–15 minutes, turning once. Remove from the pan. Add the sugar to the fat in the pan and cook until caramelised, then add the curry paste and cook for few minutes until fragrant. Stir in the coconut milk and half a can of water. Simmer and stir until everything is combined, then add the fish sauce and lime leaves.

2 Slip in the duck legs, cover the pan and cook in the oven for 1½ hours. The curry can be prepared up to 2 days ahead and left in the fridge.

3 Put the pan back on the heat, add the pineapple and simmer for 2 minutes. Adjust the seasoning, adding more fish sauce for salt and more sugar for sweetness. Stir through half the chilli and half the Thai basil leaves, if using, pour over the duck, then scatter with the rest of the chilli and basil. Serve with rice.

PER SERVING 659 kcals, protein 38g, carbs 20g, fat 49g, sat fat 20g, fibre 2g, sugar 18g, salt 2.29g

Brazilian chicken with spicy tomato & coconut sauce

As everyone gets their own chicken breast this dish is an easy one to adapt depending on the number of guests.

❄ • **TAKES 1 HOUR** • **SERVES 6**

2 onions
small chunk fresh ginger
2 garlic cloves
1 red chilli
2 tbsp olive oil
6 boneless skinless chicken breasts
400g can chopped tomatoes
200ml carton coconut cream
4 tbsp chopped coriander, to sprinkle
2 limes, cut into wedges, to garnish

1 Peel and roughly chop the onions, ginger and garlic. Halve, deseed and chop the chilli. Put all these ingredients into a food processor and work to a paste.
2 Heat the oil in a large pan, add the chicken and fry until lightly browned on both sides. Remove from the pan. Add the onion paste and fry for 10 minutes, stirring, until the onions are softened. Stir in the tomatoes and some salt and pepper to taste, then bring to the boil.
3 Add the chicken and simmer, covered, for 15 minutes. Add a splash of water if the sauce becomes too thick. Stir in the coconut cream and cook for 5 minutes until the chicken is tender. The chicken can now be cooled and chilled, or frozen for 3 months – defrost before reheating.
4 To serve, sprinkle with coriander and serve with wedges of lime, accompanied by basmati rice that's been cooked with a few saffron strands and a green salad.

PER SERVING 328 kcals, protein 37g, carbs 8g, fat 17g, sat fat 11g, fibre 1g, sugar 6g, salt 0.36g

Baked salmon & aubergine cannelloni

This smart twist on lasagne is perfect for relaxed entertaining. You can either chill the uncooked dish overnight, or else freeze it for up to 3 months. Defrost before cooking.

❄ • **TAKES 2 HOURS** • **SERVES 6**

2 tbsp olive oil
2 onions, halved and sliced
2 aubergines, sliced and diced
1kg carton passata
200ml/7fl oz dry white wine
3 tbsp capers
1 tbsp caster sugar
500g tub mascarpone
300ml/½ pint milk
145g tub fresh pesto
3 eggs, beaten
6 salmon fillets, skinned
12 sheets fresh lasagne
2 × 400g bags spinach leaves
50g/2oz Parmesan, grated
basil leaves, to garnish

1 Heat the oil in a large pan and fry the onions until turning golden. Stir in the aubergines, then fry for 5 minutes. Pour in the passata and wine, then stir in the capers, sugar, 1 teaspoon salt and some black pepper. Cover. Cook for 20 minutes.
2 Spoon 250g/9oz of the mascarpone into a bowl with the milk, pesto and eggs, and beat until smooth. Halve each salmon fillet to make two long pieces. Spread 1 tablespoon of the remaining mascarpone over each pasta sheet, add a piece of salmon, then season and roll up.
3 Wash and wilt the spinach in a large pan then squeeze dry. Spread on the base of a large lasagne dish. Arrange the salmon and lasagne on top, then pour over the tomato and aubergine sauce then top with the pesto and mascarpone.
4 To cook, heat oven to 190C/170C fan/gas 5, sprinkle over the Parmesan and bake for 40 minutes. Leave for 5–10 minutes before scattering with basil.

PER SERVING 1,074 kcals, protein 51g, carbs 41g, fat 78g, sat fat 36g, fibre 7g, sugar 23g, salt 2.79g

Braised beef with horseradish potatoes

The meat and potatoes are frozen together in this dish, which makes it really easy to serve.

❄ • **TAKES 2 HOURS** • **SERVES 8**

3 × 500g packs lean diced braising
   steak
4 tbsp plain flour
3 tbsp olive oil
8 fresh bay leaves
2 × 330ml cans stout
1 beef stock cube
400g/14oz shallots, peeled
400g/14oz baby button mushrooms
3 carrots, cut into chunky sticks
200ml tub crème fraîche
600ml/1 pint milk
3 tbsp horseradish sauce
1.25 kg/2lb 12oz potatoes, peeled
   and thinly sliced

1 Lightly dust the beef with the flour. Fry in batches in the oil in a large pan until browned, then return all the meat to the pan with 2 bay leaves. Pour over the stout and crumble in the stock cube. Part-cover and simmer for 1¼ hours.
2 Add the shallots, mushrooms and carrots, season well, then cook for 30 minutes, stirring occasionally. Tip into a large, shallow ovenproof dish and cool.
3 Meanwhile, tip the crème fraîche, milk and horseradish into a large pan and bring to the boil. Add the potatoes and remaining bay leaves, season, then simmer on a low heat for 10 minutes, stirring frequently until the potatoes are almost tender. Leave to settle for 5 minutes, then pile on top of the beef, bay leaves and all. The dish can now be chilled for up to 3 days or frozen for up to 6 weeks. Thaw completely in the fridge before reheating. To serve, bake at 190C/170C fan/gas 5 for 40 minutes.

PER SERVING 646 kcals, protein 51g, carbs 45g, fat 28g, sat fat 12g, fibre 5g, sugar 12g, salt 1.08g

Cheesy celeriac, potato & bacon pie

To make this pie veggie, omit the bacon and use vegetarian cheese. The uncooked pie can be made a day ahead or frozen for 1 month – just defrost before baking.

❄ ● **TAKES 1 HOUR 20 MINUTES**
● **SERVES 8**

2 small or 1 large celeriac, peeled, halved and sliced
2 large potatoes, sliced
150ml pot double cream
few rosemary sprigs, leaves chopped
2 × 500g packs puff pastry
150g/4oz Gruyère, finely sliced
4 rashers smoked streaky bacon, cut into small chunks
1 egg, beaten

1 Heat oven to 200C/180C fan/gas 6. Put the celeriac and potatoes in a large pan, cover with salted water and bring to the boil. Turn down the heat and simmer until just tender. Drain, then toss with the cream, rosemary and some seasoning

2 Roll one block of pastry until just bigger than a dinner plate, cut into a circle and put on to a baking sheet. Leaving a 3cm/1¼in border, spread out a layer of celeriac and potatoes, top with some cheese and bacon, then repeat the layers until all the ingredients are piled up.

3 Roll out the second block of pastry large enough to cover the bottom sheet and filling with some overhang. Brush the bottom border with a little of the egg, then drape the pastry sheet over, pushing down to seal the edges. Trim off the excess and crimp the edges.

4 Pierce a hole in the top of the pie, brush with the remaining egg and score the pastry lightly. Bake for 25 minutes then stand for 5 minutes before serving.

PER SERVING 690 kcals, protein 16g, carbs 44g, fat 51g, sat fat 26g, fibre 7g, sugar 4g, salt 2.05g

Duck au vin

This delicious take on a bistro regular can be made up to 2 days ahead and reheated to serve, or can be frozen for up to 3 months if completely defrosted before heating.

❄ ● **TAKES 2½ HOURS** ● **SERVES 6**

6 duck legs
4 tbsp plain flour
1 tbsp sunflower oil
3 carrots, chopped
1 onion, chopped
4 garlic cloves, roughly chopped
1 bottle cheap red wine
tied bundle thyme and bay
140g/5oz smoked bacon lardons
200g/7oz baby button mushrooms

1 Heat oven to 180C/160C fan/gas 4. Tip the duck into a bowl and season. Scatter over the flour and toss until coated. Heat the oil in an ovenproof casserole dish with a lid and spend 10 minutes browning the duck on all sides. Remove the duck, then add the carrots, onion and garlic and cook for 5 minutes until starting to colour.
2 Nestle the duck among the veg and pour over the wine. Add the herbs, season, then bring everything to the boil. Cover with the lid and put in the oven for 1½ hours. If you're chilling or freezing the dish, then allow it to cool. Lift the duck into a container, strain the sauce into another and chill both. Once chilled, scrape any fat from the sauce.
3 To serve, heat the cleaned dish and sizzle the lardons for 5 minutes. Turn up the heat, add the mushrooms and cook for 3–4 minutes. Return the duck and sauce to the dish and simmer for 10 minutes until heated through and the sauce has reduced a little.

PER SERVING 642 kcals, protein 41g, carbs 13g, fat 44g, sat fat 12g, fibre 2g, sugar 5g, salt 1.33g

Fish pie with saffron mash

If the prawns in this warming dish haven't been frozen before, you can freeze the uncooked pie for 1 month, defrosting in the fridge before cooking.

❄️ • **TAKES 1¾ HOURS** • **SERVES 6**

FOR THE FILLING

3 shallots, finely chopped
150ml/¼ pint white wine
142ml pot double cream
800g/1lb 12oz spinach leaves (about 2 bags)
900g/2lb fresh haddock fillets, skinned and cut into chunks
200g bag raw peeled prawns

FOR THE TOPPING

pinch saffron strands
3 garlic cloves
1 red chilli, halved and deseeded
200ml/7fl oz milk
1.25kg/2lb 12oz potatoes, cut into large chunks
4 tbsp olive oil

1 Tip the shallots and white wine into a pan, put on the heat and reduce until practically dry. Add the cream, bring to the boil, then simmer gently until reduced by two-thirds. Leave to cool.

2 Tip the spinach into a colander and pour over boiling water. Cool under the cold tap, then squeeze dry. Set aside.

3 For the topping, mash the saffron, garlic and chilli together. Tip into a pan with the milk, bring to the boil, then remove from the heat. Bring the potatoes to the boil and simmer for 15 minutes until soft. Drain, then mash well with the saffron milk and olive oil.

4 To assemble the pie, mix the fish and prawns into the cold cream. Tip into a large dish. Unravel the spinach and lay it over the fish, then top with the mash.

5 To cook, heat oven to 200C/180C fan/gas 6. Cook the pie for about 30 minutes until golden and starting to brown and bubble at the edges.

PER SERVING 683 kcals, protein 51g, carbs 42g, fat 35g, sat fat 15g, fibre 6g, sugar 7g, salt 1.36g

Proper beef, ale & mushroom pie

For the best results, make the stew in advance and keep in the fridge for up to 2 days, or the freezer for 3 months – then simply defrost and assemble the pie to cook.

❄ • **TAKES 4 HOURS** • **SERVES 6**

2 tbsp vegetable oil, plus extra for greasing
1kg/2lb 4oz braising steak
2 large onions, roughly chopped
4 large carrots, chopped into large chunks
4 tbsp plain flour, plus extra for dusting
300ml/½ pint dark ale
2 beef stock cubes mixed with 400ml/14fl oz boiling water
200g/7oz smoked bacon, lardons or chopped rashers
200g/7oz chestnut mushrooms, halved
flour, for dusting
2 × 375g blocks shortcrust pastry, rolled into a ball
1 egg yolk, beaten, to glaze

1 Heat oven to 160C/140C fan/gas 3. Heat half the oil in a casserole, brown the meat, then set aside. Add the veg to the pan and cook until coloured. Add the flour and tip the meat back into the pan. Pour over the ale and stock, and bring to a simmer. Cover and cook for 2 hours.

2 Heat a drop of oil in a frying pan and sizzle the bacon. Turn up the heat, add the mushrooms and cook until golden. Stir into the stew and leave to cool.

3 To make the pie, heat oven to 220C/200C fan/gas 7. Grease a pie dish and dust with flour. Roll out two-thirds of the pastry to a round that will line the dish with an overhang. Brush the overhang with egg yolk. Add the beef to the dish, reserving some of the gravy.

4 Roll out the remaining pastry to a lid and cover the pie. Trim the edges and crimp the pastry. Brush with egg, make a hole in the centre and bake for 40 minutes until golden. Leave to rest for 10 minutes and heat up the reserved gravy.

PER SERVING 1,244 kcals, protein 54g, carbs 105g, fat 70g, sat fat 29g, fibre 7g, sugar 15g, salt 2.61g

Cherry, almond & lemon mascarpone tart

Round off an idyllic afternoon by presenting this impressive dessert and feel doubly smug, as it's totally make-ahead.

TAKES 1¾ HOURS ● SERVES 8

375g block dessert pastry
flour, for dusting
about 700g/1lb 9oz cherries, stoned

FOR THE FRANGIPANE MIX

100g/4oz unsalted butter at room
  temperature
100g/4oz golden caster sugar
100g/4oz ground almonds
1 egg

FOR THE MASCARPONE MIX

2 × 250g tubs mascarpone
zest and juice 1 lemon
140g/5oz icing sugar, plus extra for
  dusting

1 Roll out the pastry on a floured surface to just thinner than a £1 coin. Use to line a 22cm-round loose-bottomed tart tin, with overhanging pastry. Chill on a baking sheet. Whizz the frangipane ingredients together in a food processor.

2 Heat oven to 200C/180C fan/gas 6 and bake the pastry blind for 20 minutes, then remove the beans, prick the base with a fork and continue to bake for 10 minutes. Spread the frangipane over the base and return to the oven for 15 minutes until cooked. Remove from the oven, trim the sides of the pastry and leave to cool completely. This can be done the night before.

3 Beat the mascarpone with the lemon zest and juice and the icing sugar – you can do this the night before. Spread over the frangipane and arrange the cherries on top. (This can be done several hours before serving.) To serve, remove from the tin and dust heavily with icing sugar.

PER SERVING 847 kcals, protein 8g, carbs 68g, fat 62g, sat fat 30g, fibre 3g, sugar 50g, salt 0.44g

Salted caramel chocolate torte

Salted caramel is a trendy dessert flavour combination and this stunning torte won't disappoint. The torte can be prepared a day ahead – keep chilled until ready to serve.

TAKES 1½ HOURS • SERVES 8

175g/6oz digestive biscuits
85g/3oz butter, melted
397g can caramel
1 tsp sea salt
600ml tub double cream
300g/10oz plain chocolate (70% solids), broken into chunks
25g/1oz icing sugar
2 tsp vanilla extract
salted caramel chocolates or chocolate truffles, to decorate

1 Line a 20cm-round loose-bottomed cake tin with baking parchment, making sure that it comes just above the sides of the tin. Crush the biscuits and stir in the melted butter, then evenly press into the bottom of the tin. Chill for 10 minutes.

2 Reserve 2 tablespoons of the caramel, then stir the sea salt into the rest and spoon into the centre of the biscuit base. Spread so the base is evenly covered but a 1cm/½in border of biscuit remains. Chill. Stir 1 tablespoon of the cream into the reserved caramel and set aside.

3 Melt the chocolate in a bowl over a pan of simmering water. Turn off the heat but leave the bowl and gradually stir in the remaining cream. Sift in the icing sugar and stir in the vanilla extract. Cool.

4 Pour the chocolate mixture around the edge, so it fills the biscuit border, sealing the caramel in the centre. Then pour in the rest. Chill for at least 5 hours.

5 Transfer to a serving plate and dot chocolates on top. Drizzle with the caramel–cream mixture and serve.

PER SERVING 925 kcals, protein 8g, carbs 74g, fat 69g, sat fat 39g, fibre 2g, sugar 61g, salt 1.27g

Passion fruit & coconut panna cotta

The classic Italian make-ahead dessert gets a tropical makeover, perfect for an intimate dinner party.

TAKES 15 MINUTES • MAKES 4

12 ripe wrinkly passion fruit
300ml pot double cream
160ml carton coconut cream
140g/5oz caster sugar
juice ½ lemon
12g sachet powdered gelatine
2 tbsp icing sugar

1 Halve six of the passion fruit and scoop out the pulp into a pan. Add the cream, coconut cream, caster sugar and lemon juice. Heat everything together, then gently boil, stirring until the sugar has dissolved. When the cream is simmering, scoop out about 100ml/3½fl oz into a small bowl and scatter over the gelatine. Stir until dissolved, stir back into the pan, then take off the heat. Press through a sieve into a jug, then pour the mixture into four mini pudding basins. Leave for at least 4 hours until completely set.

2 Meanwhile, halve and scoop the rest of the passion fruit through a sieve into a bowl. Mix to sweeten with the icing sugar, add 1 tablespoon of the seeds from the sieve back into the sauce, then stir to mix. Everything can be made up to 2 days in advance and chilled.

3 To serve, briefly dip the moulds into hot water until they just loosen at the sides, then invert on to serving plates. Spoon the sauce around the plates and serve.

PER SERVING 434 kcals, protein 3g, carbs 46g, fat 27g, sat fat 17g, fibre 2g, sugar 45g, salt 0.15g

Iced trifle slice

A traditional trifle doesn't hold well on a hot summer's day, so freezing it first is the perfect solution. It can be frozen for up to 1 month.

❄ • **TAKES 20 MINUTES** • **SERVES 6–8**

2 tbsp toasted flaked almonds
100ml/3½fl oz condensed milk
300ml/½ pint double cream
1½ tbsp sherry
1 tsp vanilla paste or extract
1 sheet leaf gelatine
400g/14oz raspberries
3 tbsp icing sugar
12 sponge trifle fingers

1 Line a 900g loaf tin with cling film, then scatter over the almonds. Divide the condensed milk and double cream between two bowls. Add the sherry to one and the vanilla to the other. Chill the vanilla then whisk the sherry until thick. Spoon the sherry cream on top of the almonds. Cover then freeze until firm.

2 Whisk the vanilla cream until thick, then spoon over the frozen sherry-cream layer. Put back into the freezer until firm.

3 Soak the gelatine in cold water. Whizz half the raspberries in a food processor with the icing sugar and 2 tablespoons water. Sieve into a pan and gently warm through. Remove from the heat, squeeze out the gelatine and add to the purée.

4 Crush half the remaining raspberries, then stir these into the purée with the whole raspberries. Cool. Spoon on top of the vanilla layer, press the sponge fingers lightly into it, then freeze until solid. Remove from the freezer 15 minutes before serving.

PER SERVING (6) 397 kcals, protein 5g, carbs 27g, fat 31g, sat fat 16g, fibre 2g, sugar 24g, salt 0.12g

Chestnut & amaretto roulade

This posh Swiss roll is bound to impress because it looks difficult, even though it's actually quite simple!

❄ **SPONGE • TAKES 1 HOUR 40 MINUTES • SERVES 6**

butter, for the tin
3 eggs, separated
140g/5oz caster sugar
250g can unsweetened chestnut purée
  or 375g/13oz peeled chestnuts
2 tbsp Disaronno
300ml/½ pint double cream
2 tbsp icing sugar

1 Heat oven to 160C/140C fan/gas 3. Butter and line a 20 × 30cm Swiss roll tin. Whisk the yolks and sugar together until thick, then fold in the chestnut purée or peeled chestnuts.
2 Whisk the whites into stiff peaks, then fold into the chestnut mixture. Pour into the greased tin and cook for 40 minutes.
3 Cool for 5 minutes, then cover with a damp tea towel and leave for an hour. Meanwhile, make your cream. Simply add the Disaronno to the double cream and whisk until thick and spreadable.
4 Take a big piece of greaseproof paper and sprinkle generously with icing sugar. Turn the roulade out on to the paper, spread the cream on and carefully roll it up tightly, starting with one of the short edges and using the paper to help. Don't worry if it cracks – it's part of the charm. The roulade can be made several hours in advance, just keep it somewhere cool.

PER SERVING 468 kcals, protein 5g, carbs 39g, fat 32g, sat fat 17g, fibre 1g, sugar 31g, salt 0.31g

Chocolate Orange & Grand Marnier truffle cake

A decadent chocolate dessert that cleverly uses shop-bought chocolate oranges. Freeze for up to 1 month, with the leftover peel frozen separately.

❄ ● **TAKES 1 HOUR** ● **SERVES 10**

1 orange
5 tbsp Grand Marnier
50g/2oz caster sugar
2 Terry's dark Chocolate Oranges, separated into segments
85g/3oz unsalted butter, softened
3 eggs, separated
284ml pot double cream
140g/5oz Rich Tea fingers
142ml pot double cream, lightly whipped
grated dark chocolate or chocolate curls, to decorate

1 Line a 900g loaf tin with cling film. Squeeze the orange and mix with 3 tablespoons of the Grand Marnier. Cut the orange peel (pith removed) into strips and boil in 300ml/½ pint water for 20 minutes. Add the sugar, then simmer uncovered until you have soft, sticky peel.
2 Melt the chocolate and beat in the butter and egg yolks, followed by the rest of the Grand Marnier. Whisk the egg whites until they hold their shape, then whip the cream until softly stiff. Fold both into the chocolate. Spoon 5 tablespoons of the chocolate into the tin. Dip the finger biscuits in the orange and Grand Marnier, and put on top. Scatter over some of the peel, then spoon on more chocolate.
3 Carry on layering until you have four layers of biscuit, finishing with a chocolate layer. You should only need to use half the peel. Cover with cling film. Freeze.
4 To serve, remove from the freezer no more than 1 hour before serving, top with whipped cream and the remaining peel, and scatter with grated chocolate.

PER SERVING 599 kcals, protein 7g, carbs 41g, fat 45g, sat fat 25g, fibre 1g, sugar 33g, salt 0.32g

Tangy lemon tart

You can dust the tart with icing sugar and caramelise with a blowtorch just before serving, but this is by no means essential.

TAKES 1½ HOURS ● SERVES 8
375g block dessert pastry
flour, for dusting
FOR THE FILLING
5 eggs
140g/5oz caster sugar
150ml/¼ pint double cream
juice 2–3 lemons (about 100ml/3½fl oz)
   and 2 tbsp lemon zest

1 To make the filling, beat all the ingredients, except for the zest, together. Sieve the mixture, then stir in the zest.
2 Roll out the pastry on a lightly floured surface to about the thickness of a £1 coin, then lift into a 23cm-round tart tin. Press down gently on the bottom and sides, then trim off any excess pastry. Stab a few holes in the bottom with a fork and put back in the fridge for 30 minutes.
3 Heat oven to 160C/140C fan/gas 3. Line the tart with foil and fill with rice or dried beans. Bake for 10 minutes, then remove the tart tin from the oven, discard the foil and rice or beans, and bake for another 20 minutes until biscuity. When the pastry is ready, remove it from the oven, pour in the lemon mixture and bake again for 30–35 minutes until just set. Leave to cool, then remove the tart from the tin. The tart can be made up to a day before. Serve at room temperature or chilled.

PER SERVING 770 kcals, protein 13g, carbs 86g, fat 44g, sat fat 24g, fibre 2g, sugar 38g, salt 0.18g

Chocolate & coffee truffle pots

What better way to finish a meal than rich chocolate truffles and coffee? This easy dessert combines the two.

❄ • **TAKES 20 MINUTES** • **MAKES 6**

200g/7oz dark chocolate
100ml/3½fl oz strong coffee
4 tbsp your favourite spirit, such as
    rum, brandy or Disaronno
400ml/14fl oz double cream
2 tbsp golden caster sugar
cocoa powder, to dust

1 Break the chocolate into small chunks and tip into a bowl with the coffee and alcohol. Bring 250ml/9fl oz of the cream to the boil, then pour over the chocolate mixture and stir until the chocolate has melted and the mixture is smooth. Divide the mix among six coffee cups and leave to set overnight in the fridge. They can be prepared 2 days in advance or frozen for 1 month – defrost completely in the fridge before serving.
2 To serve, whip the remaining cream with the sugar until just set. Spoon the cream on to the chocolate pots and serve dusted with cocoa powder so each cup looks like a cappuccino.

PER POT 543 kcals, protein 3g, carbs 28g, fat 45g, sat fat 25g, fibre 1g, sugar 27g, salt 0.04g

Frozen blueberry & lime cheesecake

If there is any of this no-cook cheesecake left over, simply put it back in the freezer as a treat for another day. It'll freeze for up to 2 weeks.

❄ ● **TAKES 30 MINUTES**
● **SERVES 12**

3 limes
50g/2oz caster sugar
250g/9oz blueberries

FOR THE CHEESECAKE

3 egg whites
140g/5oz icing sugar
250g tub mascarpone
½ tsp vanilla extract
300ml tub double cream

FOR THE BASE

250g box soft amaretti biscuits,
    broken up into crumbs
50g/2oz butter

1 Line a 20–22cm- square cake tin with cling film. Finely grate the zest from the limes and set aside. Squeeze the juice and pour into a pan with the sugar and blueberries. Gently dissolve the sugar, then simmer until the blueberries are softened. Remove and set aside the berries. Boil the juice for 1–2 minutes, then pour over the blueberries and cool.

2 Whisk the egg whites until stiff, then gradually whisk in the icing sugar. Beat the mascarpone in a bowl with the lime zest and vanilla. Whip the cream until it just holds its shape, then fold into the mascarpone. Fold in the egg whites.

3 Melt the butter and add to the biscuit crumbs. Mix well. Spoon the blueberries and their juices into the base of the prepared tin. Spoon the cheesecake mixture evenly over the top. Spoon over the amaretti crumbs evenly, pressing down. Freeze.

5 Before serving, transfer the cake to the fridge for 30 minutes. Serve upturned.

PER SERVING 407 kcals, protein 3g, carbs 37g, fat 28g, sat fat 16g, fibre 1g, sugar 26g, salt 0.38g

Black Forest trifle

This updated version of two classic puds in one will feed a crowd but takes very little time to prepare.

TAKES 30 MINUTES • SERVES 8

500ml tub ready-made chilled custard
100g/4oz plain chocolate, broken into
   pieces
400g/14oz shop-bought chocolate
   brownies
2 × 390g jars cherries in kirsch or
   similar
300ml tub double cream
200ml tub crème fraîche
25g/1oz icing sugar
grated chocolate and fresh cherries
   (optional), to decorate

1 Put the custard into a pan with the chocolate pieces. Gently heat, stirring, until the chocolate has melted into the custard. Cover with cling film and cool.
2 Arrange the brownies in the base of a trifle bowl. Drain the jars of cherries, reserving the liquid, and scatter over the brownies. Drizzle over 100ml/3½fl oz reserved liquid. Spoon the cooled chocolate custard over and chill while you make the topping.
3 Lightly whip the cream with the crème fraîche and icing sugar until soft peaks form. Everything can be prepared to this stage the day before and chilled until ready to serve.
4 To serve, pile the cream on top of the trifle and decorate with grated chocolate and fresh cherries, if you like.

PER SERVING 723 kcals, protein 7g, carbs 62g, fat 52g, sat fat 31g, fibre 2g, sugar 55g, salt 0.34g

Créme caramel

Once you have mastered the caramel, this light but indulgent dessert is surprisingly easy to make. It will keep in the fridge for up to 3 days.

TAKES 40 MINUTES • MAKES 6

500ml/18fl oz milk
3 large eggs, plus 2 egg yolks
100g/4oz caster sugar
a few drops vanilla paste or extract
2 tbsp Cointreau or Grand Marnier
  (optional)

FOR CARAMEL

140g/5oz caster sugar
3 tbsp cold water

1 Put the sugar for the caramel in a small frying pan and add the water. Heat slowly, stirring until the sugar has dissolved. Increase the heat and allow to bubble – do not stir. Watch carefully and when it starts to turn golden at the edges, swirl (don't stir!) the pan to ensure even colouring. When it is a rich golden colour, remove from the heat.

2 Heat oven to 160C/140C fan/gas 3. Pour the caramel into six ramekins. Bring the milk to simmering point and put the eggs and yolks in a bowl with the sugar and whisk lightly together. Gradually whisk in the hot milk. Strain into a jug and add the vanilla and liqueur, if using. Pour carefully into the prepared ramekins.

3 Pour boiling water into a roasting tin to come halfway up the sides of the ramekins. Bake for 15–20 minutes. Leave to cool, then chill.

4 To turn out each caramel, run a sharp knife around the top of each ramekin, put a dessert plate on top and invert. Give a shake and remove the ramekin.

PER CARAMEL 267 kcals, protein 8g, carbs 46g, fat 7g, sat fat 2g, fibre none, sugar 46g, salt 0.21g

Strawberry mousse cake

The texture of this cake is lighter than a cheesecake, so make sure it's well set before cutting. It can also be served frozen on a hot day.

❄ ● **TAKES 50 MINUTES**

● **SERVES 8–10**

175g/6oz digestive biscuits
75g/2½oz butter, melted
400g/14oz white chocolate
400g/14oz strawberries
300g tub full-fat soft cheese
200ml/7fl oz double cream

1 Crush the biscuits with a rolling pin to fine crumbs, add the melted butter and mix well. Tip the mix into a lined 20cm-round, loose-bottomed cake tin, smooth with the back of a spoon and put in the fridge for 30 minutes.

2 Melt 375g/13oz of the chocolate in a microwave or bowl set over a pan of simmering water, then allow to cool slightly.

3 Take out six nice-looking strawberries and set aside. Blitz the remaining strawberries in a food processor until smooth, then add them to a bowl with the soft cheese and cream. Beat until really smooth and thick, then stir in the melted chocolate. Pour on top of the biscuit base and smooth the top. Put in the fridge and chill overnight.

4 Halve the reserved strawberries and place on top of the cheesecake. Melt the remaining chocolate and drizzle over the top. Keep chilled until ready to serve.

PER SERVING (8) 737 kcals, protein 8g, carbs 47g, fat 59g, sat fat 35g, fibre 2g, sugar 35g, salt 0.89g

Gooseberry cream & elderflower jelly pots

Gooseberries have to be the most underused British summer berry, so why not rediscover them with these lovely little jelly pots.

TAKES 25 MINUTES • MAKES 6

300g/10oz green gooseberries, topped and tailed
100g/4oz caster sugar
600ml/1 pint double cream
2 gelatine leaves
100ml/3½fl oz elderflower cordial

1 Put the gooseberries in a frying pan with 25g/1oz of the caster sugar and gently heat until tender, but not pulpy.
2 Put the cream and remaining sugar into a small pan, boil, then simmer for 3 minutes. Take off the heat and stir in the gooseberries and any pan juices. Divide the mix among six glasses and chill until they firm up – about 2 hours.
3 To make the elderflower jelly, soak the gelatine in a little water. Warm the cordial in a small pan – when you see it steaming, remove from the heat. Squeeze the gelatine leaves to remove the excess water, then stir into the hot cordial until they are completely melted. Add 100ml/3½fl oz cold water, then transfer to a small jug.
4 Carefully pour a layer of the jelly mix on top of each glass of gooseberry cream – get the jug as close as possible so you don't disturb the cream. Transfer the little pots to the fridge and chill for at least 3 hours or until the jelly is set.

PER POT 616 kcals, protein 4g, carbs 31g, fat 54g, sat fat 30g, fibre 1g, sugar 31g, salt 0.08g

Foolproof chocolate fondants

These melt-in-the-middle fondants really are foolproof – just make sure you set your timer so they don't overcook.

❄ **UNCOOKED** ● **TAKES 30 MINUTES**
● **MAKES 6**

175g/6oz butter, plus extra melted
    butter for greasing
cocoa powder, for dusting
175g/6oz good-quality dark chocolate
200g/7oz golden caster sugar
4 eggs
85g/3oz plain flour
vanilla ice cream, to serve

1 Heat oven to 200C/180C fan/gas 6. Use a pastry brush to grease six dariole moulds or individual pudding basins really well and put in the fridge for the butter to set. Then grease again, dust with cocoa powder and set aside.

2 Melt the butter and chocolate in a bowl set over a pan of barely simmering water, then remove. In a separate bowl, beat the sugar and eggs until light and fluffy. Fold the chocolate and beaten egg together, then finally fold through the flour.

3 Divide the mixture among the darioles. The puddings can now be chilled for up to 2 days or frozen for 1 month and cooked from frozen. Put on a baking sheet and bake for exactly 12 minutes from chilled or 15 minutes from frozen until the mixture has puffed up and formed a crust but still has a slight wobble to it. Turn the puddings out on to serving plates with ice cream.

PER FONDANT 635 kcals, protein 9g, carbs 60g, fat 42g, sat fat 23g, fibre 2g, sugar 44g, salt 0.52g

Coconut, raspberry & lime meringue slice

All the elements to this light dessert are make-ahead and can be assembled an hour before serving. The meringues can be made 1 day in advance, or frozen for 1 month.

❄ **MERINGUE** ● **TAKES 1¾ HOURS**
● **SERVES 8**

5 egg whites
300g/10oz caster sugar
2 tsp cornflour
2 tsp white wine vinegar
85g/3oz desiccated coconut
a little flaked coconut
300ml/½ pint double cream
50g/2oz icing sugar
zest and juice 2 limes
200g/7oz raspberries

1 Heat oven to 140C/120C fan/gas 1. Line baking sheets with baking parchment and draw three rectangles, 25 × 12cm. Whisk the egg whites until stiff. Gradually whisk in the sugar to stiff, then the cornflour and vinegar. Fold in the desiccated coconut and pipe, or spread, the meringue mix evenly on to the three rectangles. Scatter the flaked coconut over one meringue and bake all three for 1 hour, then turn off the oven and leave inside with the door shut for 1 hour. Cool.
2 Whisk the cream, icing sugar, lime zest and juice to a thick consistency – this can be done a day ahead and chilled. Spread half over one meringue base (not the flaked coconut one – save that for the top), and scatter over half the raspberries. Sit the second meringue base on top, spread with the remaining cream and scatter with the remaining raspberries. Top with coconut-covered meringue and serve.

PER SERVING 434 kcals, protein 3g, carbs 46g, fat 27g, sat fat 17g, fibre 2g, sugar 45g, salt 0.15g

Almond & apricot sundaes

Just 10 minutes to make, these simple little trifle sundaes are the perfect end to a traditional Sunday roast.

TAKES 10 MINUTES • MAKES 4

1 shop-bought Madeira loaf cake, cut into cubes
8 tbsp Disaronno
2 × 410g cans apricots, chopped and juice reserved
500g pot fresh custard
300ml/½ pint double cream
2 tbsp toasted flaked almonds

1 Line the bottom of four small glass serving dishes with the cake. Mix half the Disaronno with 6 tablespoons of the reserved apricot juice, then divide this among the bowls. Arrange the apricots on top of the liqueur-soaked sponge, then pour on the custard. Cover and chill for at least 10 minutes, or up to a day.
2 Just before serving, add the remaining Disaronno to the cream and whip until it just holds its shape. Spoon the cream over the custard and sprinkle with flaked almonds.

PER SUNDAE 1,017 kcals, protein 10g, carbs 99g, fat 62g, sat fat 34g, fibre 3g, sugar 77g, salt 0.97g

Malt chocolate cheesecake

This crowd-pleasing dessert is completely make-ahead, so all you have to do on the night is take it out of the fridge and bask in the glory.

TAKES 1 HOUR • SERVES 10

200g/7oz malted milk biscuits, crushed
    to crumbs
100g/4oz salted butter, melted
5 tbsp caster sugar
2 × 300g tubs full-fat soft cheese
300ml pot double cream
300g/10oz white chocolate, melted
200g bar milk chocolate, melted
2 tbsp malt or Horlicks powder
37g bag white Maltesers

1 Line the base and sides of a deep 22–23cm-round loose-bottomed baking tin with baking parchment. Mix the biscuits, melted butter and 2 tablespoons of the sugar, then press into the base. Chill while you make the filling.

2 Divide the soft cheese and cream evenly between two bowls. Add the white chocolate to one, and the milk chocolate, malt and remaining sugar to the other. Beat each with an electric whisk until smooth.

3 Spread the milk-chocolate mixture evenly in the tin. Wipe round the edge to give a smooth edge. Spoon the white-chocolate mix over the top and gently smooth. Decorate with Maltesers and chill for at least 5 hours until firm. Can be made up to 2 days ahead.

PER SERVING 782 kcals, protein 9g, carbs 53g, fat 60g, sat fat 33g, fibre 1g, sugar 46g, salt 1.01g

Index

Also available from BBC Books and *Good Food*

Baking
Cakes & Bakes
Chocolate Treats
Cupcakes & Small Bakes
Easy Baking Recipes
Fruity Puds
Teatime Treats
Tempting Desserts

Easy
30-minute Suppers
Budget Dishes
Cheap Eats
Easy Student Dinners
More One-pot Dishes
One-pot Dishes
Simple Suppers
Speedy Suppers
Slow Cooker Favourites

Everyday
Best-ever Chicken Recipes
Best-ever Curries
Fish & Seafood Dishes
Hot & Spicy Dishes
Italian Feasts
Meals for Two
Mediterranean Dishes
Pasta & Noodle Dishes
Picnics & Packed Lunches
Recipes for Kids
Storecupboard Suppers

Healthy
Healthy Eats
Low-fat Feasts
More Low-fat Feasts
Seasonal Salads
Superhealthy Suppers
Veggie Dishes

Weekend
Barbecues and Grills
Christmas Dishes
Delicious Gifts
Slow-cooking Recipes
Soups & Sides

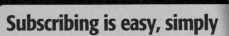